The Future
of Christian Learning

The Future
of Christian Learning

An Evangelical
and Catholic Dialogue

Mark A. Noll and
James Turner

Thomas Albert Howard, editor

Brazos Press

a division of Baker Publishing Group
Grand Rapids, Michigan

© 2008 by Thomas Albert Howard

Published by Brazos Press
a division of Baker Publishing Group
P.O. Box 6287, Grand Rapids, MI 49516-6287
www.brazospress.com

Printed in the United States of America

Library of Congress Cataloging-in-Publication Data
Noll, Mark A., 1946–
    The future of Christian learning : an Evangelical and Catholic dialogue /
  Mark A. Noll and James Turner ; Thomas Albert Howard, editor.
      p. cm.
    ISBN 978-1-58743-213-2 (pbk.)
    1. Learning and scholarship—Religious aspects—Christianity. 2. Evangeli-calism—Relations—Catholic Church. 3. Catholic Church—Relations—Evan-gelicalism. I. Turner, James, 1946– II. Howard, Thomas A. (Thomas Albert), 1967– III. Title.
BR115.L32N65 2008
280′.042—dc22   2007046986

Contents

I

Introduction

By Thomas Albert Howard

The present volume grew out of a dialogue held on the campus of Gordon College in Wenham, Massachusetts, on September 25, 2006. That such a dialogue on such a topic between a leading American evangelical scholar and a leading American Catholic scholar would take place at an evangelical college in the heart of New England reflects changes that have been and remain afoot.

Permit a brief reflection on place and history.

Despite the association today of Boston with things Irish and Catholic, New England, it should be remembered, was an inhospitable place for Roman Catholicism to put down roots. Even as it did, the region witnessed more than its share of Catholic-Protestant tensions. Like much else in American history, it perhaps all started in 1620 with the *Mayflower*, when William Brewster lugged across the Atlantic an English translation of the Venetian historian Paulo Sarpi's venomous attack on the Council of Trent and the institution of the papacy.

Subsequent generations of Puritans, both in the Old World and in the New, raised denunciations of "Popery" into an art form. A glance at Harvard's book index from the seventeenth and eighteenth century reveals titles such as "The Papists detected, and the Jesuits subtill practises to ruin and subvert the nation, discovered and laid open" (1678); "Popery: the grand apostasie" (1680); and "Papists no Catholicks, and popery no Christianity" (1685). For New England children, "Break the Pope's Neck" was a popular fireside game, while the *New England Primer* (where the young learned their ABCs and rudimentary moral lessons) reminded its impressionable readers to "Abhor that arrant whore of Rome, / and all her blasphemies."

When significant numbers of Catholic immigrants actually arrived in New England in the nineteenth century, things got more complicated and volatile; anti-Catholic invective adjusted its rhetoric accordingly. For at this time in the new nation's history, not only did Catholics represent an abiding affront to true Christianity but their hierarchical organization and ties to Rome made them an "enemy from within," a threat to republican values such as liberty, democracy, and independent thought. Apostate Christians, Catholics were also sorry Americans. For a period in the 1850s the virulently anti-Catholic Know-Nothing Party actually controlled the Massachusetts state legislature, which held its sessions in a city where a Protestant mob had torched an Ursuline monastery in 1834. Boston was also the site of the so-called Eliot School Rebellion, a tense stand-off between Catholics and public school officials over the compulsory daily reading of the (Protestant King James) Bible.[1]

1. For much of the above I am indebted to John T. McGreevy, *Catholicism and American Freedom* (New York: W. W. Norton, 2003), 8–15, and Mark S. Massa, SJ, *Anti-Catholicism in America: The Last Acceptable Prejudice* (New York: Crossroad, 2003), 18–58.

When Europe's unwashed masses arrived in even greater numbers in the late nineteenth century, Protestants felt their longstanding proprietary stake in the region truly under siege. The Baptist minister Adoniram Judson Gordon (1836–95), the founder of what is now Gordon College and a man of considerable piety and virtue, was not untouched by powerful anti-immigrant currents of nativism and anti-Catholicism. Labeling the papacy a "monster of blasphemy," Gordon also worried that the "evil hand of the Jesuits would be felt upon the throat of our Republic" if something were not done to stem Catholic immigration.[2] Such sentiments were hardly isolated; they expressed a widespread consensus of anti-Catholicism among American evangelical Christians in the late nineteenth and early twentieth century.[3]

But if American Protestants of various stripes worried about superstitious masses and scheming priests infiltrating the country, Catholics on both sides of the Atlantic had long expressed puzzlement and contempt at the revivalist, populist forms of Protestantism that appeared to thrive in the context of American freedoms, frontier expansion, and the new land's capitalist ethos. For the English Catholic Hilaire Belloc, the American political experiment in general and the revivalist enthusiasms of American Protestants in particular tended to create "a spiritual condition peculiar to that Continent,"

2. Quoted in Scott M. Gibson, *A. J. Gordon* (Lanham, MD: University Press of America, 2001), 154–55. On the galvanizing and unifying effects of anti-Catholicism on Boston's conservative Protestants, see Margaret Lamberts Bendroth, *Fundamentalists in the City: Conflict and Division in Boston's Churches, 1885–1950* (New York: Oxford University Press, 2005).

3. See John Wolffe, "Anti-Catholicism and Evangelical Identity in Britain and the United States, 1830–1860," in *Evangelicalism: Comparative Studies of Popular Protestantism in North America, the British Isles, and Beyond, 1700–1900,* ed. Mark Noll, David Bebbington, and George A. Rawlyk (New York: Oxford University Press, 1994), 179–97.

which produced "[a] quite unique experiment in the religious field." The "strictly voluntary" nature of religion in America, Frenchman Achille Murat wrote, leads to a "thousand and one sects which divide the people of the United States. Merely to enumerate them would be impossible, for they . . . evince nothing stable but their instability." While the neo-Thomist philosopher Jacques Maritain had much positive to say about America, he too worried that sectarianism, biblical literalism, and unreflective cultural accommodation might undermine serious Christian intellectual life there. Such conditions "can develop a cast of mind which, in the intellectual field, would mean a horror of any tradition, the denial of any lasting and supra-temporal value." [4] As noted later in this volume, the Vatican had even felt pressed, on the cusp of the twentieth century, to condemn a vague phenomenon called "Americanism," which some European Catholic critics associated with the deformation of true belief under the political conditions of the United States.[5]

But that was then . . . If the nineteenth and much of the twentieth century was marked by a skeptical stand-off between American Catholic and evangelical Christians, nourished by bitter memories and entrenched habits of thought, recent decades have witnessed a warming of relations and indeed some points of truly momentous spiritual and intellectual conciliation. Elsewhere, Mark Noll has argued

4. The quotes are taken from Martin E. Marty, "Experiment in Environment: Foreign Perceptions of American Religion," *Journal of Religion* 56 (1976): 291–315.

5. See Gerald P. Fogarty, SJ, *The Vatican and the American Hierarchy from 1870 to 1965* (Collegeville, MN: Liturgical Press, 1985), 143–94.

that a "minor revolution" in improved Catholic-evangelical relations has occurred since the late 1950s.[6] One should not exaggerate the extent of the thaw, and here is not the place to narrate reasons for its occurrence. Still, the essays and responses that follow might be helpfully viewed in light of at least a few developments.

The significance of the Second Vatican Council (1962–65) and the historic papacy of John Paul II cannot be overstated. The Council's decrees on religious freedom (*Dignitatis Humanae*) and ecumenism (*Unitatis Redintegratio*), in particular, have helped make possible what past generations deemed unthinkable. The former decree, in my view, amounts to a forceful, theologically adroit embrace of the very principles of religious freedom that have long contributed to evangelicalism's flourishing in this country, while the latter boldly proclaims that "both sides were to blame" for the breach of the sixteenth century and that greater cooperation and dialogue with "separated brethren" is essential. The Council elaborated: "We must come to understand the outlook of our separated brethren. Study is absolutely required for this, and should be pursued with fidelity to truth and in a spirit of good will. . . . Of great value for this purpose are meetings between the two sides, especially for discussion of theological problems, where each can deal with the other on an equal footing."[7] The current volume might even be understood as a modest effort—on the topic of Christian higher education—to give concrete expression to the Council's sentiment.

6. Mark Noll, *American Evangelical Christianity: An Introduction* (New York: Oxford University Press, 2001), 17. Cf. William M. Shea, *The Lamb and the Lion: Evangelicals and Catholics in America* (New York: Oxford University Press, 2004).

7. Austin Flannery, OP, ed., *Vatican Council II*, vol. 1, *The Conciliar and Postconciliar Documents*, rev. ed. (Northport, NY: Costello, 2004), 461.

As is well known, John Paul II made Rome's "irrevocable" commitment to the ecumenical venture a significant focus of his papacy, seeking deeper understanding particularly with Eastern Orthodoxy but also with the various "ecclesial communities" that trace their roots to the Protestant Reformation. Wisely warning against a "false irenicism" that papers over abiding differences, the pope nonetheless lamented the Church's "deplorable divisions" and noted that "complacency, indifference and insufficient knowledge of one another often make this situation worse." Of special interest for our purposes, he called attention to the theological climate in the United States, "where one notices a great ecumenical openness."[8]

Indeed, ecumenical ventures and various informal nexuses of interconfessional cross-pollination in the United States between evangelical Christians and Catholics have developed from a negligible trickle to a noteworthy stream. Inspired both positively and negatively by earlier ecumenical efforts among mainline Protestant denominations, evangelical Christians have begun to emerge from their particularist enclaves—many of which reflect the unfortunate institutional fallout from the modernist-fundamentalist controversies of the early twentieth century. Resolved to avoid, or at least learn from, the decline and internecine struggles of the mainline churches, evangelicals nonetheless have increasingly recognized that "the docetic, Gnostic, and Manichaean tendencies" (Noll) inherited from fundamentalism only vex and oppress a vital Christian witness, especially for those convinced that the doctrines of Creation and Incarnation not only allow but mandate serious intellectual and cultural

8. *Ut Unam Sint* (1995), available at http://www.vatican.va/holy_father/john_paul_ii/encyclicals/documents/hf_jp-ii_enc_25051995_ut-unum-sint_en.html.

expression. Accordingly, a number of evangelical theologians, such as D. H. Williams, have called for a deeper engagement with ancient, creedal Christianity, a "retrieving the tradition" for the purposes of "renewing evangelicalism."[9] Or as the Methodist theologian Thomas Oden has put it, "For too long, evangelicals have remained distanced from many of the classic themes of orthodoxy. . . . Much of this distance is now being closed by interaction between evangelicals and Eastern Orthodox, and between evangelicals and Catholics."[10] At the same time, a longstanding, fruitful meeting of minds between evangelicals and (Kuyperian) Reformed Christians has produced a scholarly phenomenon of significant influence and national visibility.

But the narrowing gap between evangelicals and more traditional expressions of the faith cannot be chalked up to evangelical intellectual *ressourcement* alone. As others have noted, it has also been powerfully abetted by broader social and cultural factors. Past Protestant-Catholic hostilities took place against a shared backdrop of general cultural religiosity. However, as more aggressive forces of secularism, scientism, and ethical utilitarianism have made themselves felt, both in the academy and in the broader public arena, erstwhile non-speaking siblings have willy-nilly found themselves cooperating on a range of policy questions and social issues, even if they might disagree on tactics, solutions, or priorities. Timothy George of Beeson Divinity School has famously referred to this reality as an "ecumenism of the trenches," the most often-cited indicator of which comes from American presidential politics. When John F. Kennedy ran for president in 1960, many evangelicals worried that

9. D. H. Williams, *Retrieving the Tradition and Renewing Evangelicalism* (Grand Rapids: Eerdmans, 1999).

10. Thomas Oden, *The Rebirth of Orthodoxy: Signs of New Life in Christianity* (New York: HarperCollins, 2003), 65.

a "papist" occupying the White House would take his cues from Rome. But during John Kerry's bid for the presidency in 2004, evangelicals often worried for *precisely the opposite reason*: why did Kerry seem out of step on many issues with the powerful and respected moral voice of John Paul II?

One could proliferate other examples of creeping conciliation, whether intellectual, theological, or social. But as these are well documented, it might be advisable—if I may leap from the descriptive to the prescriptive—to let another line from Timothy George sum up where matters stand: "For faithful evangelicals and believing Roman Catholics, this is a time to sew, not a time to rend."[11]

As an institution shaped by the evangelical tradition, Gordon College has come to recognize the validity of George's sentiment, even if the college's various constituents might evince varied responses to it. The current publication is one of several projects at Gordon that have sought to foster dialogue and understanding across the unhappy divisions of Christianity. In recent years, for example, Gordon College has begun a relationship with neighboring St. Anselm's College, a Benedictine institution, for the purpose of shared fellowship and intellectual exchange. Faculty members at St. Anselm's and Gordon have cooperated on several conferences: one on evangelical and Catholic approaches to the "liberal arts idea," another on "Christians in Unity not Uniformity," which brought scholars, clergy, and laypeople together to reflect on ecumenical possibilities, not just in the theological heights but in the pew and on the street.

11. Timothy George, "Between the Pope and Billy Graham," in *Pilgrims on the Sawdust Trail: Evangelical Ecumenism and the Quest for Christian Identity*, ed. Timothy George (Grand Rapids: Baker Academic, 2004), 137.

The college recently hosted a conference entitled "Highly Favored: A Symposium on Mary across Christian Traditions," a discussion among Protestant, Catholic, and Orthodox representatives on the place of the Virgin Mary in theology and worship.[12]

Some of these endeavors, including the current volume, were supported by a grant from the Lilly Endowment on the Christian idea of vocation, which we titled "Critical Loyalty: Christian Vocation at Gordon College."[13] I serve as the overall project director. The title of the project, to coin a phrase, says it all. "Critical Loyalty" reflects a conviction-driven, tension-filled dual sensibility felt by many at the college: a desire to remain fiercely loyal to the special gifts (proclamation of the gospel, concern for the needy, soulful hymnody, devotion to scripture, inter alia) found abundantly in the evangelical tradition; at the same time, a recognition that some contemporary manifestations of evangelicalism, especially in relation to the life of the mind and engagement with Christian tradition, have left much to be desired. In responding to the current shape of evangelicalism, the college recognized that "evangelical higher education now finds itself at a crossroads" as it seeks to address three constructive criticisms in particular:

> First is . . . the contention that evangelical Christians all too often have been inadequate stewards of the mind. . . . Second, while evangelicals have placed great emphasis on individual study and application of Scripture (worthy goals in themselves), they have sometimes done so at the expense of knowledge of and participation in the broader tradition

12. The majority of these events were hosted by Gordon College's Center for Christian Studies (http://www.gordon.edu/ccs).

13. Emeritus Professor Malcolm Reid of Gordon College's philosophy department should get credit for coining the title.

of Christian thought and reflection. . . . Finally, critics have questioned evangelicals for standing aloof from ecumenical engagement. . . . In sum then, anti-intellectualism, wariness of tradition, and a tepid concern for ecumenism, we contend, have unfortunately compromised the evangelical movement in contemporary America and diminished its understanding of Christian vocation.[14]

In many respects, the current volume, and the conference from which it derived, touch upon all three issues: intellectual engagement, tradition, and ecumenism. The basic idea behind the project was to bring to Gordon's campus a leading American evangelical scholar and a leading American Catholic scholar, both familiar with their own tradition, with one another's tradition, and with the general landscape of "Christian learning," understood to mean what goes on at actual institutions of higher education, as well as the broader world of academic scholarship. Once this goal was formulated, two names quickly leapt to mind: Mark Noll and James Turner—scholars whom I have long suspected might be American reincarnations of the (irenic, erudite) Protestant reformer Philipp Melanchthon and the (irenic, erudite) Catholic humanist Desiderius Erasmus. Indeed, the pairing seemed perfect, for not only were both highly respected scholars able to meet the aforementioned criteria, but they taught at institutions that (at least to a considerable degree) reflected some of their deepest theological commitments—Wheaton College and the University of Notre Dame, respectively.

As planning processes got under way, however, Mark Noll accepted an endowed chair at Notre Dame, bringing

14. "Critical Loyalty: Christian Vocation at Gordon College," grant proposal submitted to the Lilly Endowment (August 29, 2002), 2. The grant narrative is available at www.gordon.edu/criticalloyalty.

his long and distinguished tenure at Wheaton to an end and thereby making among his first tasks in his new post a toe-to-toe encounter with his new colleague and (then-serving) departmental chair, James Turner! Thus our dialogue lost the symbolism of confessionally contrasting institutions, even as we retained the intellectual firepower of the invitees. As readers will discover, those in attendance were rewarded with a heady mix of hard-earned erudition, theological commitment, and gracious eloquence—all focused on what I am persuaded are among the more interesting and consequential developments in recent decades: points of (promising) contact and (lingering) conflict between evangelical and Catholic approaches to higher education and scholarship.

As one will see, punches were not withheld, but neither were any thrown below the belt. And while much ground was covered, it should be clear at the outset that neither interlocutor presumed the impossible task of speaking for the whole "evangelical tradition" or "Catholic tradition." Rather, both self-avowedly represent a particular voice within these traditions at a particular moment of their development. Their words here ought to be interpreted as a snapshot, interpretative summary of a fast-moving story of Tolstoyian complexity, the contours of which suggest broad implications for the shape of Christian higher education, for the future of ecumenical relations, and for American intellectual and religious life generally.

Christian learning in the United States, to be sure, encompasses far more than evangelical and Catholic vantage points. If one had world enough and time, a conversation of this sort should go on for days and include Eastern Orthodox, Pentecostals, Mennonites, Anglicans, Lutherans, and so on. The dialogue presented here thus should be understood to represent only one facet—albeit not an insignificant one—of a much larger and more complex conversation.[15] Furthermore, it should be borne in mind that both Noll and Turner are trained as historians, something that invariably affects the form and content of their analyses. A dialogue on "Christian learning" between an Orthodox theologian and a Mennonite sociologist, in other words, would yield another, presumably very different outcome.

Nevertheless, Noll and Turner set about their tasks quite differently. In his essay Noll takes a more *diachronic* approach, assessing the current situation and future possibilities by tracing theological disparities and conflicting habits of thought back to the sixteenth-century breach. By contrast, Turner offers a more *synchronic* approach, examining more contemporary configurations and developments. Even so, some of their conclusions strikingly converge and reflect a growing, if by no means unanimous, consensus among Christian scholars and educators: that past fixities are no longer fixed, that many erstwhile theological certainties are no longer certain, and that out of the many-layered confusions, realignments, and surprise turnabouts of the present, hopeful, if inchoate and challenging, opportunities present themselves. Neither Noll nor Turner pulls out that overworked whipping boy "postmodernism" to explain or denounce current reconfigurations, nor do they wax nostalgic about a time when Catholic and evangelical scholars operated in more isolated, self-confident intellectual subcultures. Rather, they advise pressing ahead together, prudently and

15. For introductions to the larger conversation, see Richard T. Hughes and William B. Adrian, eds., *Models for Christian Higher Education: Strategies for Success in the Twenty-first Century* (Grand Rapids: Eerdmans, 1997), and Paul Dovre, ed., *The Future of Religious Colleges: Proceedings of the Harvard Conference on the Future of Religious Colleges, October 6–7, 2002* (Grand Rapids: Eerdmans, 2000).

hopefully. As Turner puts it, speaking of the fragmentation of knowledge in the academy, "If designers of college curricula are ever . . . to find a collective ground of discourse, ever, in short, to give voice again to the silenced unity of knowledge, they will do so only by thinking in terms of a new intellectual tradition that evangelicals and Catholics alike can share." Whether or not this is possible is anyone's guess, he concedes; perhaps "all one can responsibly conclude is that change is in the air and the future of Christian learning is open ended."

Noll strikes a similar note of inconclusivity and guarded optimism, stressing the importance of evangelicals and Catholics' actively seeking common ground and providing mutual assistance. "Although they have moved through very different historical trajectories," he suggestively opines, "American Catholics and American evangelicals now find themselves in the strange position of being able to offer to each other a gift out of their own resources that responds to a need manifest in the other." "A new day has dawned" for Christian learning, he believes, one "big with implications—for younger scholars choosing research strategies and discovering their own natural faith communities, for older scholars both drawn to and skittish about new possibilities across the Catholic-evangelical border . . . and, not least, for deans, provosts, presidents, and trustees of Christian institutions. If the latter do what they should do, they must balance faithfulness to their institutions' particular traditions with aggressive exploitation of the deeper Christian possibilities opened up by Catholic-evangelical engagement."

Most who pick up this book, I imagine, desire deeper Christian possibilities, however variously this phrase may be understood. That is my desire too. My hope then is that this slim volume will raise helpful questions, promote deeper insights, and, regardless of one's background or convictions, demonstrate that one need not return to thirteenth-century Paris or sixteenth-century Wittenberg to observe *fides quaerens intellectum* of a high order.[16] Behold, you hold evidence that it has happened in the twenty-first century, *between* an evangelical Protestant and Catholic scholar—and *in* New England.

I would like to offer a special word of gratitude to the Lilly Endowment and its Program for the Theological Exploration of Vocation (PTEV) for supporting this and other endeavors of the Critical Loyalty project at Gordon College. I am grateful too for the Lilly Committee at Gordon College, the members of which have consistently demonstrated abundant faithfulness, patience, goodwill, and sharp intelligence. In particular, I thank Chris Carlson, Greg Carmer, Kina Mallard, Daniel Russ, Mark Sargent, Bruce Webb, and Daniel White.

Kirsten Heacock, Kirstin Hasler, and Stephen G. Alter generously read portions of the manuscript and helped me with my editing task, while my wife, Agnes R. Howard, proved, once again, to be an invaluable interlocutor and constructive critic during the whole process.

Finally, I owe a special debt to Sarah and Andrew Carlson-Lier, whose highly competent assistance quite simply made the on-campus dialogue and this publication possible.

16. The specific venue within the Critical Loyalty Project that brought Noll and Turner to campus was in fact titled the Faith Seeking Understanding lecture series.

II

The Essays

Reconsidering Christendom?

By Mark A. Noll

The Western Christian world—and with it, Western Christian learning—may be said to have split in two at 6:00 p.m. on the evening of April 15, 1521, in the presence of the assembled Diet of the Holy Roman Empire in a small city of about seven thousand inhabitants just south of Mainz, Germany. When at the Diet of Worms the Augustinian friar Martin Luther rejected a demand from representatives of the pope and the emperor to retract opinions he had published concerning the damage being done to Christian faith by the Roman Catholic Church,

> I ask by the mercy of God, may your most serene majesty, most illustrious lordships, or anyone at all who is able, either high or low, bear witness, expose my errors, overthrowing them by the writings of the prophets and the evangelists.... Unless I am convinced by the testimony of the Scriptures or by clear reason (for I do not trust either in the pope or in councils alone, since it is well known that they have

often erred and contradicted themselves), I am bound by the Scriptures I have quoted and my conscience is captive to the Word of God. I cannot and I will not retract anything, since it is neither safe nor right to go against conscience.[17]

Immediately after hearing these words, Johann Eck, the secretary of the Holy Roman emperor, fired right back with a speech that is much less famous than Luther's but was in its way just as prescient as Luther's testimony was revolutionary:

You [Luther] revive those [errors] which the general Council of Constance, composed of the whole German nation, has condemned, and you wish to be refuted by means of Scripture. In this you are completely mad. For what purpose does it serve to raise a new dispute about matters condemned through so many centuries by church and council? Unless perhaps a reason must be given to just anyone about anything whatsoever. But if it were granted that whoever contradicts the councils and the common understanding of the church must be overcome by Scripture passages, we will have nothing in Christianity that is certain or decided.[18]

The next day, April 19, the twenty-one-year-old emperor, Charles V, who reigned over more of Europe than any monarch since the days of Charlemagne, wrote out in his own hand a letter to the German Diet. In it he recounted his descent from "most Christian emperors," all of whom "remained up to death faithful sons of the church," and then he expressed his firm conviction about what he had recently

17. "Luther at the Diet of Worms," trans. Roger A. Hornsby, in *Luther's Works*, vol. 32, *Career of the Reformer II*, ed. George W. Forell (Philadelphia: Fortress, 1958), 112.
18. Ibid., 113.

witnessed: "I am determined to support everything that these predecessors and I myself have kept, up to the present, and especially what has been laid down by these my predecessors at the Council of Constance as well as others." As for Martin Luther, "it is certain that a single friar errs in his opinion which is against all of Christendom and according to which all of Christianity will be and will always have been in error both in the past thousand years and even more in the present."[19]

In the momentous exchange of April 1521, the key contrast for the future of Christian learning lay between Luther's profession that his conscience was captive to the Word of God and Charles's insistence that the opinions of a single friar could not be allowed to stand "against all of Christendom." A conception of Christian existence in which "conscience" loomed large was being posed against a conception of Christian existence in which "Christendom" occupied a central place.

This contrast did not lead immediately or inevitably to the cataclysmic effects that antagonists at Worms anticipated. The Catholic Church, which Luther felt was laying waste so many souls, soon reformed itself quite thoroughly, though not, to be sure, in accord with Luther's prescriptions. The Protestant movements that came out of Luther's protest, which Johann Eck and Charles V saw as fatally embracing a principle of individualism, did not completely abandon trust in inherited truths and comprehensive church institutions. Even since the eighteenth century, when Protestant individualism has come closer to fulfilling Catholic fears, the principles of scripture and reason that Luther enunciated have maintained more ecclesiastical cohesion than Catholics considered possible.

19. Ibid., 144n9.

Yet the divisions of the Reformation era were still very real. In order to know Christ, liberate scripture, and obtain salvation, Luther and his Protestant successors would be willing to transform the functioning institution of the visible church into an increasingly abstract notion of an invisible church. In order to experience Christ, maintain the authority of scripture, and obtain salvation, Charles V and his Catholic successors would insist upon the functioning institution of the visible church as an essential keystone of genuine faith. Today, North American evangelicals and Catholics are heirs of these sixteenth-century inclinations: evangelicals as decisively formed by an individual appropriation of scripture, Catholics as decisively formed by an inherited commitment to the visible church.

But also today, it is easy to see that North American evangelicals and Catholics have been shaped by much else that transpired in the nearly half-millennium since the events of April 1521. That history has framed Christian learning as much as have the contrasting religious impulses at work among Protestants and Catholics. Today when we consider Christian learning, it is necessary to take account of the rise of modern science, the Enlightenment and the eighteenth-century discovery of the individual, the expansion of democratic liberalism, the rise of the modern research university, the effects of colonization-decolonization and the world wars, as well as the emergence of affluent consumerism alongside the realities of multicultural pluralism—not to speak of the powerful legacies associated with figures such as Bacon, Descartes, Locke, Newton, Voltaire, Rousseau, Jefferson, Darwin, Marx, Nietzsche, Freud, Einstein, Margaret Sanger, and Foucault. In Christian perspective, all these movements and people were created and providentially overseen by God; if we have Christian learning in view, each represents an

Egypt to selectively despoil as well as an Egypt from which to flee.

To think about Catholicism, evangelicalism, and Christian learning means, therefore, to confront immense complexity: concerning the internal histories of both religious traditions, concerning the relation of those internal histories to the worlds of learning, concerning the tangled ligaments of modern intellectual life, and concerning the presence (or absence) of Christian influence in the various branches of human learning today. As a possible contribution toward managing this complexity, I would like to explore three theses, the first mostly conceptual, the latter two mostly historical.

1. Christian learning worthy of the name must, by the nature of the case, involve both real learning and real Christianity.
2. Christian learning has flourished in the circumstances of what I shall call a revived Christendom.[20]
3. Because of recent developments within Catholicism, within evangelicalism, and within American intellectual culture, American Catholics and evangelicals, in order to advance the cause of Christian learning, now have special need for what each offers the other.

1. Christian learning worthy of the name must, by the nature of the case, involve both real learning and real Christianity.

20. This claim—indeed, this entire essay—concerns what has happened in the West. It is possible that the same dynamics do not apply for Christian learning within the Orthodox world or among the world's many new indigenous Christian movements.

In making this claim I understand "real learning" to mean curiosity and openness toward human and natural phenomena, healthy self-criticism about the intellectual assumptions treasured by one's particular tribe, a strong commitment to empirical research as a way of modifying or even overturning inherited certainties, and a humble determination to benefit from as wide a community of learners as possible. These qualities have been widely touted as ideals in the modern research university, where they have also been known sometimes actually to function. But even though functioning never means living up to the ideal, where these ideals have been actualized even partially, genuine learning has occurred.

Christian learning worthy of the name must be as genuinely Christian as genuinely learned. Here I take "real Christianity" to mean a trinitarian understanding of God, and also of the world as fully understandable only in relation to the Trinity. Real Christianity, in these terms, acknowledges God as creator and providential sustainer of all that exists; it looks upon Christ as the only effective agent for the salvation of humankind, which has denied its own creaturely status by turning away from God; and it regards the Holy Spirit as the active presence of God in the world whose task, in the words of John's Gospel, is to "convince the world of sin and of righteousness and of judgment" (16:8).

For evangelical Protestants the hurdles standing in the way of Christian learning worthy of the name can be described as super-spiritual docetism, sectarian gnosticism, and partisan Manichaeism.[21] According to J. N. D. Kelly, docetics in the early Christian centuries "disparaged matter and were

---

21. In what follows, I recapitulate material explored in somewhat greater length in *The Scandal of the Evangelical Mind* (Grand Rapids: Eerdmans, 1994), 52–56.

disinterested in history," and so they "were prevented from giving full value to the fundamental Christian doctrine of the incarnation of the Word."[22] When evangelicals sing "This world is not my home" and when we treat the daily round of ordinary existence as unworthy of diligent attention because of our fixation on supposed spiritual realities, we display a docetism that undercuts Christian learning. The same is true with the evangelical propensity to set great store by in-group interpretations of general scriptural themes or specific biblical passages. When such interpretations ignore the counterweight of Christian tradition or the balance of contemporary Christian consultation, they reflect a gnosticism that is fatal for Christian learning. Likewise, when evangelicals define the world as simply a stage for combat between good and evil, when we assign ourselves a Godlike monopoly on truth, and when we forget that even those who mock God are precious creatures made in the divine image, we lapse into Manichaeism. By so doing we also destroy the openness to be taught by all others that is essential for true learning.

Characteristic Catholic problems are, it seems to me, just the reverse. At least in the United States since the Second Vatican Council, Catholic tendencies may have moved too strongly in reaction to docetism, gnosticism, and Manichaeism. Common Catholic temptations strike me as offering too much respect for nature as created and too little attention to the operations of divine grace in redeeming the world, as emphasizing catholicity too strongly and being skittish about reasoning directly from scripture as divine revelation, and showing too great a willingness to find truth, beauty, and goodness distributed at large in a world riddled with sin and death.

22. J. N. D. Kelly, *Early Christian Doctrines* (New York: Harper, 1978), 27–28.

If I may generalize, evangelicals characteristically fall short of Christian learning because their Christianity is too *sharp*, Catholics because their learning is too *broad*.

Against both kinds of excess, Christian learning worthy of the name reflects the balance that is central to the Christian faith itself. That balance was expressed preeminently in the Chalcedonian formula that presents Christ as fully human and fully divine in one integrated person, but it is also found in a classical understanding of scripture as thoroughly a product of human composition and also an entirely trustworthy revelation from God. It is seen in an attitude toward humanity that features both the desperate human need for rescue and the universal human claim for respect—or, as stated once by Father Theodore Hesburgh, "the deep, agelong mystery of Salvation in history" combined with "the inner, inalienable dignity and rights of every individual human person."[23]

Christian learning should be marked by both audacity and humility, by a willingness to challenge paradigms reigning in the world and a willingness to admit mistakes pointed out by its strongest "enemies" in the world. It must combine great openness and tight particularity, genuine contingency and genuine certainty. It is driven by a need for the churches to teach the world and a need for the churches to learn from the world. Without such balance, attempts at Christian learning can only stagger and spin; they will not go anywhere.

But of course Christian learning looks different depending on what is being studied. Most problems in the physical world will be approached the same way by a believing physicist and a nonbelieving colleague. The same holds for

23. Theodore M. Hesburgh, CSC, introduction to *The Challenge and Promise of a Catholic University* (Notre Dame, IN: University of Notre Dame Press, 1994), 8.

much historical scholarship—for example, about warfare, economic developments, or presidential elections—and also in much empirical political science. To understand why physics, chemistry, biology, even evolutionary biology will look similar for all students is to realize something about the nature of creation: what is the point of elaborate contextual reflection if the explicit basis of a discipline is to study the physical world that God has made and providentially maintains? Doxology at the beginning and end of research might mark off the believer from the secularist, but not much in the actual carrying out of research.[24]

A distinctly Christian contribution is more likely to appear when believers study the history of science, or the history of world religions (including Christianity), or normative political science. In short, when foundational commitments in ethics, epistemology, and metaphysics play an obvious role in shaping and interpreting research, the Christian factor in Christian learning becomes more salient.

Whether I have construed things correctly or not, this understanding of "Christian learning" is what I will now deploy for sketching a broad outline of Western intellectual history since the Middle Ages and then a more concentrated account of the recent past.

2. Christian learning has flourished in the circumstances of a revived Christendom.

By "Christendom" I mean a society in which the institutions of an inherited and respected visible Christian church provide the main ordering principles for education, culture, and much else; where government defers to the church for

24. I am indebted to Nicholas Wolterstorff for this insight.

matters concerning family, personal morality, culture, and education; and where, in turn, the institutions and personnel of a Christian church provide legitimization for governments that carry out what are considered God-ordained tasks of preserving social stability and perpetuating the favored social position of the visible church. At Worms, Charles V was referring to this kind of society when he spoke of Christendom. As a vision in the West, Christendom had existed from the time of Charlemagne; as a system with genuine Christian effects, Christendom had actually been realized in flashes during the High Middle Ages, especially in the thirteenth century of Francis of Assisi and Thomas Aquinas; as a system with at best marginal Christian effects but strong institutional inertia, Christendom was a powerful force in the sixteenth century. Thereafter, the Christendom ideal long survived as an official stance of the Catholic Church. In fact, it was probably not until 1929, when the church finally abandoned the effort to reclaim the papacy's lost Italian territories and proclaimed an official end to the pope's status as "prisoner of the Vatican," that the Catholic Church finally moved away from the medieval ideal of Christendom that Charles V evoked.

It must be stressed that many aspects of Christendom fell woefully short of what observers today, whether believers or not, would define as normative Christianity. In particular, the use of state-sanctioned coercion to compel religious observance and constrain legitimate freedom was a persistent defect that on many occasions and in many places fatally undermined the supposed Christianity of Christendom.

In addition, especially after the sixteenth century, many competing forces greatly weakened the specifically Christian character of Christendom—including the rise of science as an autonomous sphere of intellectual authority, the hubristic claims of the Enlightenment, the comprehensive schemes of absolutist rulers, the anticlericalism of the French Revolution, the Napoleonic reshuffling of European nation-states, the rise of liberal democracy, and the transfer of authority for European universities from the churches to the nation-states. Yet so deeply entrenched were the instincts of Christendom that even when Catholicism finally abandoned its pursuit, the church kept habits of comprehension, community, proprietorship, and universality that powerfully sustained the effects of Christendom even without its actual structure.

Christendom ideals and practices were not, however, restricted to Catholics but were also taken for granted in most of the Protestant traditions that came out of the Reformation. The initial Protestant alternative to Catholic Christendom was not religious voluntarism or individualism of a modern sort but an effort to replicate Christendom on a national instead of international scale. Thus Saxony—with, later, Prussia and Scandinavia—became a Lutheran Christendom; Geneva, Scotland, and the Netherlands became Calvinist Christendoms; England became an Anglican Christendom.

These Protestant regimes long followed the principle of *cuius regio, eius religio* (the religion of the prince determines the religion of the whole population). Within their national spheres, they also simply assumed that publicly supported, exclusive church establishments should play a major role in all of society—whether defining moral norms, tending to the sick and indigent, supporting the actions of rulers, managing substantial amounts of real estate, or maintaining universities.

The great change in Protestant history that took place in the late seventeenth century on the Continent and during the eighteenth century for the English-speaking world weakened Christendom practices but did not extinguish them altogether. That change resulted from pietistic and evangelical challenges to the Protestant established churches—challenges that resembled the earlier Protestant challenges to late medieval Catholicism. The new reformers once again argued that formal, inherited, traditional religion had become stagnant; it was as much a hindrance to true Christianity as a help. The solution was again to stand *coram Deo*, to experience the demands and promises of God directly, and to be inspired by personally appropriated faith to active service in the world. But by the eighteenth century, with secular themes of the Enlightenment reinforcing the individualism of pietistic and evangelical religion, the challenge to the corporate character of Protestant Christendoms as they had descended from the sixteenth century was even stronger than the earlier Protestant challenge had been to Catholic Christendom. The era's leading pietists and evangelicals at first worked for the renewal of the established churches—Spener, Francke, and Zinzendorf as Lutherans; the Wesleys and Whitefield as Anglicans; Jonathan Edwards as a state-church Congregationalist. But then several of them set up voluntary reform societies within the established churches (Moravians, Methodists) or, like Edwards, advocated standards of church membership that moved toward separation. Finally, some of the reform societies, like the Moravians and the Methodists, hived off as denominations of their own, while others like the Baptists embraced separatism boldly by following the logic of Edwards's appeal for a church membership constituted only by professed saints. Not all pietists and evangelicals went this far, but for those who did, the result was a decisive break with Christendom—in order to rescue the personal reality of the gospel, reformers would give up the vision of a comprehensive, institutionalized Christian influence on all of society. By the middle of the eighteenth century, a few radical evangelicals were even beginning to agitate against the formal establishment of one church by the state, which had always been the keystone of historical Christendom.

That appeal for the separation of church and state was of course most fully answered in the creation of the United States, where, after a generation of constitutional experiment, the practice of state recognition and state support of one Christian denomination was abandoned, and with it the central apparatus of Christendom. States would no longer fund the churches; churches might still exert an influence over society, but only in competition with one another and only through voluntary means and by persuasion, rather than by formal laws and institutions.

In Europe, a more abrupt, harsher, and blood-drenched break from the past followed shortly after the beginning of the American experiment. Leaders of the French Revolution violently threw over the state church institutions and tried to replace them with non-Christian substitutes. Napoleon's subsequent conquest of Europe included a self-conscious assault on the institutions of historical Christendom, not least by dissolving most of the universities heretofore under Catholic or Protestant sponsorship or re-creating them as secular arms of the state.[25]

And yet . . . In both the United States and Europe, habits of Christendom died hard, even under the combined assault of evangelical separatism, the United States' republican democracy, and Napoleon's militant Enlightenment nationalism. The Congress of Vienna of 1815 restored much of the *ancien régime*, including of course many forms of Christendom. Because of the success of conservative reac-

25. My thanks to Robert Sullivan, head of the Erasmus Institute at the University of Notre Dame, for a primer on this point.

tions after Napoleon, some of Europe's church-connected universities, like Anglican Oxford and Cambridge, were able to limp along for another generation or two as institutions of Christendom. In Germany, creative innovations secured at least a modest place for something like traditional theology in the new-modeled national universities.[26] And there was space enough in some Catholic regions for renewed foundations like the Catholic University of Louvain to attempt an intellectual reconstitution of Christendom.

But the major effect of all-out Thermidorean reaction to violent revolutionary assault was a tumultuous century of *Kulturkampf*. Conflicting aspirations for social hegemony led first to sharp clashes between the historic churches and secular republicans, then to battles between church and socialists, and, finally, to the death struggle between Catholics and Marxists. The depth of European attachment to instincts of Christendom is revealed by the fact that the strongest opponents of the European state churches tried to substitute antichurch comprehension, antichurch community, antichurch proprietorship, and antichurch universality for the ideals and institutions of Christian Europe.[27]

The story in the United States was more evolutionary than revolutionary but still testified to the power of ancient ideals. When Alexis de Tocqueville visited the United States in the early 1830s, he marveled that, in the absence of Christendom's structures, Christian belief and practice flourished and with a noteworthy influence on society. He recorded the success of Protestant churches within the

26. On this entire process, see the masterful account in Thomas Albert Howard, *Protestant Theology and the Making of the Modern German University* (Oxford: Oxford University Press, 2006).

27. For a provocative account of modern European Marxism as an anti-Christian Christendom, see Hugh McLeod, *Religion and the People of Western Europe, 1789–1989*, 2nd ed. (New York: Oxford University Press, 1998).

free market created by the new American polity that grew from the churches' ability to re-create some of the effects of Christendom through democratic and liberal means. Especially Episcopalians, Congregationalists, and Presbyterians—that is, the denominations that had enjoyed Christendom status in the Old World as well as in the New World during the colonial period—were sustaining some results of Christendom without the traditional European means by securing Protestant-influenced laws and setting up Protestant-sponsored voluntary societies for many purposes. By the 1830s, they were particularly effective in starting Protestant-sponsored "public" schools where mandated daily readings from the King James Version of the Bible were defined as a nonsectarian practice and therefore enforced as the law of the land in a country that had outlawed church establishments.[28] The Protestant churches were also busy restoring a free-market type of intellectual Christendom by founding theological seminaries and sponsoring most of the nation's other institutions of higher education.

The strategy that nineteenth-century American Protestants employed to preserve effects of Christendom without the apparatus of Christendom rested on a particular set of attitudes and on an ability to secure funds. Proprietary instincts, a respect for tradition, an internal compulsion to provide social welfare, and aspirations to control society with democratic means were the attitudes. Money raised through eleemosynary channels allowed Protestants to replace governmental funding with voluntary income as a way of maintaining the effects of Christendom in a liberal democratic society that had abandoned the forms of Christendom.

28. On the conundrums this situation posed for Catholics, see the opening pages of John T. McGreevy, *Catholicism and American Freedom: A History* (New York: W. W. Norton, 2003).

In the late nineteenth century, there arose a specifically religious challenge to this American substitute for European Christendom. This challenge came from some evangelical Protestants who, like their reforming predecessors in the early sixteenth century and the early eighteenth century, were motivated by what they saw as a spiritually decayed Christendom.

Specific fundamentalist objections to mainline Protestantism often took shape as a critique of Christendom-like features of the dominant denominations. Fundamentalists, for example, held that the proprietary instincts of older Protestants led to capitulation before secular trends in the modern university: older Protestants showed far too much deference to secular ideas like evolutionary naturalism and the higher criticism of scripture that had become prominent in the leading universities they themselves had founded, funded, and led; the pursuit of knowledge in these universities seemed to be passing beyond all Christian bounds as the Protestant sponsors and beneficiaries of these universities stood by and did nothing.[29] Fundamentalists also criticized the comprehensive pretensions of the older Protestantism as expressed in the Social Gospel: perhaps it was commendable for the churches to care for needy bodies as well as eternal souls, but fundamentalists saw concentration on this-worldly concerns as driving out concern for the life to come. As the Western world came into increasing contact with African, Asian, and Oceanic civilizations, fundamentalists worried as well about the universality of the older Protestantism. It might have been acceptable to note a few commendable features of these non-Western civilizations,

29. Here I borrow insights from George M. Marsden, *Fundamentalism and American Culture* (New York: Oxford University Press, 1980), and *The Soul of the American University: From Protestant Establishment to Established Nonbelief* (New York: Oxford University Press, 1994).

as prominent representatives of liberal Protestantism and universities sponsored by the liberal Protestants did, but not if it meant cutting the nerve of missionary efforts to preach the gospel of a unique salvation in Jesus Christ. That result, however, was exactly what fundamentalists perceived as flowing naturally from the liberal Protestant emphasis on the universal fatherhood of God.

The fundamentalist critique of proprietary Protestantism was reminiscent of the original Protestant critique of proprietary Catholic Christendom at the start of the sixteenth century and of pietistic and evangelical critiques of Protestant Christendoms at the turn of the eighteenth. In all three cases, the perception of spiritual decay led to protests against the structures of church life harboring the decay. As before, the protests led to the creation of new agencies and institutions. Fundamentalist institutions of higher learning such as Gordon College,[30] Wheaton College, and the Moody Bible Institute, which defined themselves in opposition to the educational mainstream, were the result. If Oberlin and the University of Michigan were selling their souls for reputation and funds, these new institutions would keep the faith.

There was, however, a significant difference. Earlier protest movements had resulted in alternative Christendoms, first through Protestant established churches, then through institutions reformed by pietists and evangelicals, and through the voluntary proprietorship of the American Protestant mainline. In the fundamentalist era, by contrast, evangelical protest against a decayed Christendom led to institutions that, at least by profession, repudiated the proprietary instincts of Christendom altogether. These new

30. Gordon College's original name was the Boston Missionary Training Institute; it was founded in 1889.

evangelical and fundamentalist reformers were going to be *separated from the world.*

And so in the wake of fundamentalist and evangelical protests against an American Protestant Christendom of proprietorship, comprehension, and universality, the effects for Christian learning were very different from what they had been at earlier times in Western history when revival movements arose to critique the spiritual decrepitude of Christendom but stayed to breathe life into the institutions of Christendom.

With its stress on the individual, the democratic, and the voluntary, nineteenth-century American Protestantism was already a weakened Christendom. The critique to which it gave birth at the end of the nineteenth century, evangelical fundamentalism, was a religion whose strongest impulses were aligned with the American practices that had already weakened Christendom rather than with those that had re-created it. That is, fundamentalists were devotees of liberal individualism, they expressed republican fears of concentrated institutional power, they were confident in the ability of every man to interpret foundational written constitutions for himself, and (in American political terms) they displayed the Democratic Party's distrust of centralized government. By contrast, the proprietary mainline churches, in order to re-create effects of Christendom, had cultivated a measure of aristocracy, an ideal of inclusive community, a distrust of the unwashed masses, and the Whig Party's trust in government to improve the quality of life. With fundamentalism, the attack on Christendom led not to its renewal but to its virtual extinction.

The bearing on Christian learning of this lengthy excursus concerning the history of Christendom and its ersatz American replacement is precisely that many of the great moments in Western Christian learning emerged out of situations when Christendom was under attack by reformers promoting religious revival but these reformers continued simply to take for granted the ideals and practices of Christendom. Those moments coincided with situations in which a vital personal piety quickened the wellsprings of true Christianity (as defined above) and a meaningful Christendom provided a natural context for true learning (as defined above).

This common pattern was established in the thirteenth century, when monastic revival infused the institutions of medieval Europe with fresh Christian vitality and an astonishing outburst of intellectual creativity. It was present on both sides of the Reformation divide in the sixteenth century, when Protestant revival led to fresh intellectual labor as well as quickened spiritual vitality at the University of Wittenberg and the Academy of Geneva: Melanchthon as preceptor of all Germany in harness with Luther, the champion of justification by faith. Among Catholics, networks of new universities and seminaries staffed by the Jesuits and other revived orders bespoke intellectual renewal as well as spiritual vigor. Stretching things only a little, it is possible to see seventeenth-century Puritanism as a revival of Christendom, as well as a spiritual revival, one that directly promoted ambitious experiments at Emmanuel College, Cambridge, and Harvard College in Massachusetts, as well as indirectly stimulated the progenitors of the scientific revolution in England. Then at the end of the seventeenth century, the foundation of the University of Halle represented a natural outgrowth of pietistic spiritual revival that led on to pacesetting study of foreign cultures, foreign languages, pharmacology, and moral philosophy—and all while August Hermann Francke cultivated church-state ties with the Prussian monarchy. Again stretching things a little, the incredible musical output of J. S. Bach may be viewed as flowing from a counter-pietistic revival of orthodox Lutheran spirituality fully engaged with the musical infrastructure of establishmentarian Protestant Christendom. Likewise, English evangelicalism in the eighteenth century was guided by John Wesley and Charles Wesley, who always respected the institutions of Anglicanism, including higher education (perhaps more than they should have done), and, in the case of Charles, reacted strongly against any effort to separate from those institutions. In America a similar evangelical energy spilled over naturally into the founding of educational institutions that would later become Princeton University, the University of Pennsylvania, and Dartmouth College. Evangelical revival also provided the inner drive for Jonathan Edwards's extraordinary intellectual achievements.[31]

What all these examples shared was a critique of inherited Christendom based on the perception of its spiritual lethargy and encouraged by a fresh commitment to classical Christian teaching appropriated individually as leading to a personally engaged Christian life. But they also shared a basic assumption that Christendom or Christendom-like structures would provide a natural context for practicing a more active, doctrinally orthodox, and engaged Christian life.

By contrast, where Christendom was attacked by political pressure or reconstituted without spiritual revival, as in the Napoleonic era, or where the reformers of Christendom no longer shared the instincts of Christendom, as with modern fundamentalism, then Christian learning was not robustly promoted or was even rejected. In sum, Christendom,

31. See George M. Marsden, *Jonathan Edwards: A Life* (New Haven, CT: Yale University Press, 2003).

however manifold its shortcomings, has historically proved to be a most propitious environment for the flourishing of Christian learning.

3. Because of recent developments within Catholicism, within evangelicalism, and within American intellectual culture, American Catholics and evangelicals, in order to advance the cause of Christian learning, now have a special need for what each offers the other.

The symmetry of this thesis can be outlined succinctly: American Catholics enjoy the legacy of Christendom, but that legacy is now confused. The confusion arises from internal changes within the church since the Second Vatican Council and from external alterations in the church's position within American society. In the midst of such confusion, the religious focus provided by evangelical revival offers the prospect not only for deepened Christian existence but also for the self-confident promotion of Christian learning.

For their part, American evangelicals are heirs to a strong revival tradition, but more and more evangelicals perceive that tradition as incomplete and distorted. The incompleteness and the distortion come from the historical imbalance of American revivalism itself; the awareness of incompleteness and distortion has grown in the last several decades especially among evangelicals who have felt called to academic vocations. In the midst of such disorientation and sense of incompleteness, the cultural depth and breadth provided by the legacies of Christendom offer the prospect not just for a helpful correction to the religious weaknesses of revivalism but also for a better promotion of Christian learning.

Although they have moved through very different historical trajectories, American Catholics and American evangelicals now find themselves in the strange position of being able to offer to each other a gift out of their own resources that responds to a need manifest in the other. This position is strange because no one fifty years ago could have guessed that some evangelicals and some Catholics would soon be regarding each other as fellow Christian believers, but it is also strange because of how recent developments in American public culture have inadvertently enabled Catholics and evangelicals to assist each other. I have treated the reasons for the unexpected but hopeful reengagement of Catholics and evangelicals elsewhere and do not need to add anything here.[32]

The American situation, however, requires further comment. Into the 1960s, American learned culture seemed fixed in its long but persistent flight away from specific Christian influence. To be sure, by galvanizing the nation morally as well as militarily, World War II had prompted an upsurge of religion. But this religion was more patriotic theism than a sharply focused particular faith. As argued persuasively in Will Herberg's penetrating *Protestant, Catholic, Jew* (1955), a generic religion of "Judeo-Christian values" easily became as much a substitute for individual faiths like evangelicalism or Catholicism as an extension of them.

Whatever the state of popular culture, university life was continuing in the secular direction that had been strengthening since the late nineteenth century. Quite apart from the intellectual self-confidence possessed by liberal democratic pragmatists, international political realists, Freudian analysts of culture, social scientists enamored of Parsonian instrumentalism, and historians of American anti-intellectualism who saw Christianity as the major culprit, the nation's organized

32. With Carolyn Nystrom, *Is the Reformation Over? An Evangelical Assessment of Contemporary Roman Catholicism* (Grand Rapids: Baker Academic, 2005).

Christian bodies did not seem positioned to offer much intellectual help. Protestant denominations such as the Lutheran Church–Missouri Synod and the Christian Reformed Church, which sustained a European respect for higher learning, as well as Eastern Orthodox communions, were locked away in ethnic enclaves. The nation's hordes of evangelicals and fundamentalists exerted almost no influence on the national intellectual agenda, partly because they had taken themselves out of this picture, partly because those who controlled that agenda did not let them in. Catholics, whatever may have been the reality within their own institutions, associations, and neighborhoods, were still regarded with nearly universal suspicion: by the acolytes of John Dewey as a threat to the pragmatist utopia, by ideological defenders of democracy and the American public school as a fifth-column of crypto-fascists, and by Protestants of many stripes as minions of the Antichrist.

Mainline Protestants were still advantageously positioned within the dominant academic culture, but apart from occasional pronouncements by figures like Reinhold Niebuhr, these Protestants made few attempts at shaping, challenging, or redirecting the nation's dominant intellectual discourse. E. Harris Harbison, an active Presbyterian who joined the history faculty at Princeton near the start of World War II, later wrote about how isolated he felt as a practicing Christian who expected his faith to inform his scholarship,[33] and this was at Princeton, the most conservative of the nation's leading universities which maintained a few of the forms of nineteenth-century proprietary Protestantism deep into Harbison's own tenure on the faculty.[34]

33. See the preface to E. Harris Harbison, *Christianity and History: Essays* (Princeton, NJ: Princeton University Press, 1964).

34. Paul C. Kemeny, *Princeton in the Nation's Service: Religious Ideals and Educational Practice, 1868–1928* (New York: Oxford University Press, 1998),

The discomfiting of the United States' once self-confident intellectual establishment which has occurred since the 1960s altered the configuration of ins and outs, and with a vengeance. The recent trials of the academy have been chronicled in a full library of books, but even a brief sketch can suggest some of the factors and forces that blew things apart. The civil rights movement and then conflict over the Vietnam War undercut assumptions about the moral indefectibility of the nation's liberal democracy. The academic elites who dominated higher education into the 1960s lost moral authority when they embraced a variety of antinationalist, avant-garde, and left-wing moral causes. A handful of brilliant historians, led by Perry Miller and then Edmund Morgan, who were often atheists or agnostics themselves, rehabilitated the reputation of the Puritans and Jonathan Edwards and showed them to be not only the most God-besotted but also the most intelligent of all early Americans. Roman Catholic firmness against communism and admiration for the nation's first Roman Catholic president, John F. Kennedy, defused much of the intellectual hauteur that had once dismissed Catholicism as unworthy of participating in the American Way of Life. From the publication of Thomas Kuhn's *Structure of Scientific Revolutions* in 1962, a host of ever-deepening challenges called into question the self-image of disinterested scientific objectivity that had once sustained the amour propre of leading scholars. Then came legions of feminists, Marxists, and multiculturalists who expanded these intellectual challenges by taking them from the ivory tower into the streets and back. Meanwhile, the obvious strength of religious forces at work in the world, and

---

and James Axtell, "God Boxes and Tribal Faiths," in his *The Making of Princeton University: From Woodrow Wilson to the Present* (Princeton, NJ: Princeton University Press, 2006), 329–44.

even the United States, gave the lie to the plot of inevitable secularization that had once comfortably reassured many American academic elites.

None of these forces or figures were particularly friendly to anything distinctly Christian, but all of them loosened the intellectual boundaries and made it harder to exclude vagrant positions, like those maintained by Catholics and evangelicals, from taking their place in the intellectual marketplace. In this new American situation there unfolded the parallel, but separate, histories of Catholic and evangelical intellectual development that, after many twists and turns, eventually brought representatives of each into contact with the other.

The Catholic story is one of sharp turning points, which can be summarized pretty quickly: crisis circa 1900 followed by remarkable achievement leading to crisis circa 1965 followed by ongoing uncertainty.

The crisis circa 1900 was occasioned by spin-off effects in the United States from papal efforts to corral theological, political, and intellectual modernism. Unlike Protestants who suffered a prolonged Fifty Years' War between fundamentalists and modernists, Catholics cut the knot swiftly by means of papal directives. The latter story is now well known in large part thanks to the superb general history by Philip Gleason.[35]

In 1899 Pope Leo XIII's papal letter *Testem Benevolentiae* condemned a shadowy collection of traits he called "Americanism." The letter attacked in particular the notion that Catholicism was unharmed when it conformed to American habits of liberty and individual expression. In

35. Philip Gleason, *Contending with Modernity: Catholic Higher Education in the Twentieth Century* (New York: Oxford University Press, 1995). Some of what follows is adapted from my essay-review of Gleason's volume in *Books & Culture* 2 (September-October 1996): 31–34.

a famous response, the archbishop of Baltimore, James Gibbons, said that he too opposed such errors but they were not found in the United States! Nonetheless, this "Americanist" controversy led Catholics to be much more cautious in following norms of American popular life.[36] The second papal statement, *Pascendi Dominici Gregis* (1907) from Pius X, represented a wholesale condemnation of "modernism." Although aimed mostly at Continental and British thinkers who were following paths marked out by Protestant liberals such as Albrecht Ritschl and Adolf von Harnack, Pius X's sweeping condemnation of modern intellectual conventions ensured that Catholic institutions in America would insulate themselves from the intellectual world that was emerging as the leading U.S. universities turned increasingly to models supplied from imperial Germany. At the same time that Leo XIII and Pius X were warning the faithful away from modern secularism, they and their successors mounted a strenuous campaign to promote the work of Thomas Aquinas as an intellectual anchor for modern Catholic intellectual life. So it was that just as American Catholics were moving from immigrant to settled communities and turning full-scale attention to their colleges and universities, they received explicit papal guidance about what they should fear and what they should foster with respect to the life of the mind.

Institutional and intellectual construction on a grand scale was the result. At the start of the twentieth century, Catholic educators made numerous tactical adjustments (like trading the European integration of prep schools and universities for the standard American division between high school and

36. The effects are clearly interpreted in R. Scott Appleby, *"Church and Age Unite!": The Modernist Impulse in American Catholicism* (Notre Dame, IN: University of Notre Dame Press, 1992).

college) that brought the forms of Catholic higher education into line with standard American patterns. But strategically, Catholic higher education set its own course, and that course moved directly against the secularizing trends of the United States' elite institutions. Especially between the world wars, Catholic colleges and universities experienced an intellectual revival marked by the promotion of neo-Thomist or neoscholastic philosophy and stimulated by a wide range of liturgical, social, and ecclesiastical reforms.

A key element of the neo-Thomist revival was confidence that the right use of reason would lead the fair-minded thinker close to what God had revealed to the church through the scriptures and the apostolic traditions guarded by the church's hierarchy. What made neo-scholasticism profoundly important in the first sixty years of this century, however, was not just its intellectual commitments but also its many links to social action, missionary service, and liturgical renewal. A shorthand indication of the power of the neo-Thomist synthesis is to note that it undergirded not only the social radicalism of Dorothy Day's Catholic Worker Movement and the widely influential philosophical personalism of Catholic Action but also the popular apologetics of Bishop Fulton Sheen and the profound reflections of John Courtney Murray, SJ, on relations between church and state. It was also the inspiration for many popular magazines, scholarly journals, and disciplinary societies—all created by Catholics for Catholics.

This enterprise was not without its problems, some of them quite serious. For some it meant authority imposed by fiat rather than authority embraced by internal conviction. Its triumphalism reflected the insecurity of immigrant communities, not unlike the way Protestant fundamentalist crusades against evolution could be expressed as masking pervasive social insecurity. The Catholic intellectual revival also led to quixotic pedagogical efforts like trying to pump a little neo-Thomism into twenty-four hundred Notre Dame undergraduates each semester during the 1950s. Moreover, in Gleason's account, the way papal dicta had resolved the modernist crisis only "reinforced the tendency toward intellectual passivity inherent in a religion that stressed authority as strongly as Catholicism did."[37]

Yet with deficiencies fully noted, it is also clear that tight papal supervision could also bring papal-inspired invigoration. This invigoration could be measured even in the discontents that luminaries of the movement ultimately expressed. Thus, the historian John Tracy Ellis in 1955 published a critique of Catholic intellectual life that played more of a role in dismantling the entire neoscholastic system than Ellis intended, but Ellis's critique owed as much to the high ideals of neoscholasticism as it did to his internalization of standards from elite American universities.[38] As president of the University of Notre Dame, Theodore Hesburgh would later play a key role in securing Catholic institutions more independence from papal control, but the great feats of intellectual midwifery that Hesburgh accomplished at Notre Dame were not conceivable apart from his nurturing in the neoscholastic revival. In the most poignant example, when after World War II John Courtney Murray's opinions on questions of church and state displeased his Jesuit superiors in the United States and the Vatican, he was ordered to stop writing on these subjects, a proscription he obeyed. Yet in retrospect it is clear that Murray's path-breaking insights into how deeply rooted religious convictions can flourish

37. Gleason, *Contending with Modernity*, 16.
38. Ellis's essay was expanded as a book, *American Catholicism and the Intellectual Life* (Chicago: Heritage Foundation, 1956).

in a democratic polity flowed directly from the church's neo-Thomism in which he was trained. In other words, the penetrating *Catholic* intelligence of John Courtney Murray is difficult to imagine outside of a church that could not through the exercise, in Gleason's words, of "raw ecclesiastical power, wielded in utter contempt of academic freedom," silence John Courtney Murray.[39]

Even if the highest ideals of the Catholic intellectual revival were never fully realized, or were only partially realized among only some of its participants, those ideals possessed, in Christian perspective, breathtaking beauty. In Gleason's summary,

> To learn more of God and God's creation was not merely to be called to apostolic action; it was to be drawn more powerfully to God as the object of contemplation, of worship, of prayer, of devotion, of the soul's desire for spiritual fulfillment. . . . The God-centeredness that was integral to Thomism, and the affective reactions it aroused, help us to understand how the philosophical dimensions of the Catholic revival—which seems, in retrospect, so often dry and mechanical—nourished, and was in turn nourished by, the literary, aesthetic, and even mystical dimensions of the revival.[40]

Put a different way, this revival amounted to a partial re-creation in a democratic environment of the comprehension, community, proprietorship, and universality of traditional Catholic Christendom.

The main problem seemed to be that no one noticed. In 1939, a symposium sponsored by Catholic educators and eventually published as *Catholics and Scholarship* bemoaned

39. Gleason, *Contending with Modernity*, 282.
40. Ibid., 122.

the fact that Catholic universities had produced, in the words of one contributor, not "a single scholar of national importance."[41] Then in 1955 part of John Tracy Ellis's indictment, "American Catholics and the Intellectual Life, " documented the lack of attention that even Roman Catholics paid to their own intellectuals.

Yet if the Catholic intellectual revival was never appreciated for what it accomplished, it was—in terms of genuine Christian learning—a remarkable effort. And in the early 1960s it collapsed as suddenly and as irrevocably as Humpty Dumpty after his great fall.

The neo-Thomist synthesis unraveled for a number of reasons, including the impact of World War II (which brought Catholic colleges and universities the benefits and the bane of government assistance), growing pressure to conform to broader secularizing patterns in American higher education, criticism of neo-Thomism from within the church itself, the unanticipated effects of the Second Vatican Council, the movement of once-immigrant Catholic communities to the prosperous suburbs, and the culture shocks of the 1960s. Since the early 1960s, the once coherent vision of Catholic intellectual life has splintered into a thousand fragments.

In the wake of that splintering, Catholic higher education, though holding its own numerically and financially, has entered into intellectual uncertainty. Most recently, the twin shocks of declining vocations and priestly sex scandals have dealt an especially severe blow to Catholic intellectual efforts. Catholic higher education had traditionally relied on priests and other religious to provide the distinctly Christian ethos of Catholic universities. Priests especially were

41. John A. O'Brien, *Catholics and Scholarship* (Huntington, IN: Our Sunday Visitor, 1939).

critical since they maintained the all-important bridge between academic subjects and the sacramental practices that defined Catholicism itself.

A Protestant observer can be pardoned for concluding that Catholic learning now reflects a bloomin' buzzin' confusion. It seems to be divided into at least three general strands, which parallel three strands in the history of American Protestant education. First are once and formally Catholic institutions that resemble once and formally Protestant institutions that have become functionally secular. Second are Catholic institutions parallel to the mainline Protestant institutions that have struggled to maintain a genuine Christian core while embracing a measure of contemporary religious pluralism; these institutions are trying to preserve distinctly Roman Catholic characteristics while also practicing a more general catholicity in pursuit of broad community service or intellectual excellence. Third are a number of mostly newer Catholic institutions that resemble at least some self-consciously evangelical institutions; they might be called sectarian because of their countercultural efforts to provide a pervasively, systematic Catholic education, or perhaps as ultramontane in their similarity to papal-oriented institutions of former centuries.

With such diversity, it is little wonder that widely varied judgments can be found on the general state of contemporary Catholic intellectual life. A German sociologist, Michael Zöller, who has spent considerable time at both Catholic and secular universities in the United States, positions himself in the moderately progressive camp that sees substantial benefit arising from the Catholic Church's adjustment to the general circumstances of contemporary American life. In his opinion, "The success story of American Catholicism is nowhere more clearly reflected than in its schools and universities, and therefore this educational achievement is the showpiece of the American church."[42]

A more nuanced but still positive view was recently offered by Nathan Hatch, as he moved to become president of Wake Forest University after a long tenure at Notre Dame. Hatch acknowledges "the struggles and failures of Catholic institutions and . . . the powerful secular undertow in academic life," yet he is also impressed with "the flourishing experiments in Catholic higher education [that he has] . . . witnessed at Notre Dame and elsewhere." In Hatch's view, American Catholic universities benefited especially from the move toward lay boards and greater independence from church authorities that came out of the Land o' Lakes Statement of 1967. Catholics have drawn resources from lay donors to improve facilities and faculties but in so doing "have not given up the dream of linking intellectual and moral purpose." In an American intellectual environment that like so much in the United States is now threatened by culture wars, Catholic institutions "provide a middle ground where vital religious traditions can engage modern thought in a climate of academic freedom . . . committed to a given point of view [and often] . . . enlivened by a founding religious community."[43]

But others have not been as optimistic. The philosopher and student of Thomas Aquinas, Ralph McInerny, also of Notre Dame, despairs at the drift he sees among Catholic elites, including the hierarchy and much of Catholic higher education. In a novel from the mid-1990s, his detective-

42. Michael Zöller, *Washington und Rom: Der Katholizismus in der amerikanischen Kultur* (Berlin: Duncker und Humblot, 1995), 235. This book has also appeared in English translation as *Washington and Rome: Catholicism in American Culture* (Notre Dame, IN: University of Notre Dame Press, 1999).
43. Nathan O. Hatch, "Intellectual and Moral Purpose Still Meet at Catholic Universities," *Chronicle of Higher Education* 51 (May 6, 2005): B16–17.

priest, Father Roger Dowling, meets a young woman from South Bend and asks her, "So you're at Notre Dame?" When she replies, "My husband is doing graduate work," and then adds, after hesitating, "In theology," Father Dowling responds, "Good God," and is prompted to wonder, "How many of those teaching theology still believe?"[44] But McInerny is not completely downcast, for he retains confidence in the piety found among individual laypeople and clerics as well as in wisdom resident in the Vatican.

Albert DiIanni, a Marist priest, was in charge of vocations in the Boston province when in 1996 he advanced a more pointed critique of Catholic universities, which in his view had "been on the defensive and suffered a failure of nerve." According to DiIanni, these universities were pursuing hiring policies focused solely on academic merit and thus had created a threat to Catholic survival: "The liberal tactic is to jettison cargo, to surrender some of the claims of Christianity, to change its content to a degree while retaining its language as a kind of mythic overlay useful for purposes of motivation. In taking this liberal route, Catholic universities did not differ much from other North American universities." His evidence for such conclusions flows from the fact that "often Catholic university graduates are not regular churchgoers and from a moral standpoint seem to have learned more from television talk shows than from the magisterium of the Church."[45]

At issue among these varying views seems to be how well the positive ideals of Christendom are faring in American Catholic higher education. Catholics generally are open to

44. Ralph McInerny, *A Cardinal Offense* (New York: St. Martin's, 1994), 37–38.

45. Albert DiIanni, "The Catholic University in a Postmodern World" (October 1996), available at http://www.catholic, net/rcc/Periodicals/Homiletic/10–96/3/3 .html.

the plentitude of God as Creator, but opinions differ as to whether that openness has overwhelmed particularistic Christian themes of holiness and judgment. Catholics are concerned about working in a proprietary manner for the good of all, but they disagree on what this proprietary attitude is costing. Catholics are unwilling to divide the needs of the body from the needs of the soul, but again controversy exists over how well Catholic intellectuals are holding together body and soul.

Compared to fifty years ago, American Catholics are more thoroughly integrated into the ways of American culture, more conscious of the need to enlist laity for the intellectual apostolate, more troubled by internal discord, more restless under papal oversight, more adept at using American patterns of voluntary fundraising, and more conflicted politically (as ancestral loyalty to Democratic concern for social needs meets newer Republican professions to speak for life and family). In sum, they are more discordant, adventuresome, conservative, progressive, innovative, modernist, integralist, faithful, and insouciant than ever.

In the midst of contemporary upheaval, Catholics, among many other urgent tasks, are seeking a way forward intellectually.

And here come the evangelicals.

By no means do I want to suggest that American evangelicals are now poised to rescue intellectual life for American Catholics. Nor is it certain that a whole lot of practical assistance is going to flow back and forth between the two groups in the foreseeable future. Yet the recent history of evangelicalism does leave it in a position to communicate with at least some parts of the Catholic world, and that communication opens the possibility for at least some Catholics to glean insight from at least some aspects of evangelical history.

The plot line of modern evangelical history is in form similar to the Catholic story, however different are the conflicts it features and the way those conflicts were resolved. In general, we see for evangelicals since the late nineteenth century, first, a break from the past leading to ghettoization, followed by increasing turmoil within the ghetto, followed by a breaking out of the ghetto, followed by a great deal of intellectual uncertainty.

The first break was the fundamentalist move toward separation, with an accompanying abandonment of the proprietary attitudes toward American culture that had been so influential in the religious history of the nineteenth century. The ghettoization was the period from roughly 1925 to 1955, when fundamentalists tried to establish a universe parallel to mainstream American culture, complete with their own communications, retreats, books, code words, styles of entertainment, and institutions of higher learning. Turmoil within this fundamentalist ghetto began in the early 1940s and grew in strength until by 1960 it was clear that significant numbers of those who had begun to call themselves evangelicals were intent on leaving the religious ghetto behind. The result, however, was not a clear-cut, well-defined, or unified evangelical program but a variable mélange of strategies, projects, voluntary efforts, lay initiatives, and innovations.

Yet the general movement of evangelical culture since the 1950s has been unmistakable. Evangelicals would not stand off but would try to mix it up.[46] A pair of key symbolic events from the mid-1950s, both involving Billy Graham, indicate the direction of this movement. In October 1956

46. This section follows Mark A. Noll, "Where We Are—and How We Got Here" (a fifty-year retrospective of American evangelicalism), *Christianity Today* 50 (October 2006): 42–49.

Graham helped launch a new periodical called *Christianity Today*. As he did so, he was deep into planning for a major evangelistic effort in New York City. Both the magazine and the campaign represent watersheds.

By assembling the personnel, hunting up the financing, and hammering away at the need, Graham was the key figure in starting *Christianity Today*. In words of an early appeal he stressed how "a religious magazine . . . that will reach the clergy and lay leaders of every denomination presenting truth from the evangelical viewpoint" could help overcome the "confused, bewildered, divided, and almost defeated" condition of evangelicals in the United States.[47] Graham's influence came from where authority has always arisen among evangelicals—from his power as a preacher. Beginning in 1944, as the first full-time employee of Youth for Christ, then through break-out campaigns in Los Angeles (1949) and Great Britain (1954), Graham had established himself as an unusually fresh, straightforward, and convincing voice for traditional evangelical faith.

That his interests also extended to a magazine such as *Christianity Today* was, however, unusual. Since the late nineteenth century, it had become customary for evangelicals to pose an antithesis between pious preaching and formal intellectual labor. Graham wanted the magazine to function differently. In a related concern, he also wanted evangelical seminary education to become more professional, a desire he translated into active support for several institutions, including Fuller Theological Seminary, Trinity Evangelical Divinity School, and Gordon Divinity School (today Gordon-Conwell Theological Seminary). By riding Graham's coattails and by their own efforts, these schools

47. Here and below, the quotations are from a 1955 speech outlining the need for such a magazine; archives, Christianity Today, Inc.

eventually became the largest American institutions of conservative Protestant theological education outside of the Southern Baptist network. Graham's hope for *Christianity Today* was that it would function as a forum uniting disparate evangelical movements but that it would also provide evangelicalism with a measure of theological depth alongside savvy social analysis. In this attempt he was joined by the founding editor of the magazine, Carl F. H. Henry, and a host of other educationally ambitious younger evangelical scholars. They shared Graham's desire for disseminating biblical expositions and evangelistic messages but also (as Graham put it) for "discuss[ing] current subjects . . . from the evangelical viewpoint," taking a stance above sectarian infighting, shunning arguments over the details of prophecy, standing "for social improvement," and advancing political opinions from the center—and all together in one place under a generic evangelical auspices. By trying to strengthen evangelicalism with biblical content brought into engagement with public issues, world affairs, and the life of the mind, *Christianity Today* marked a new evangelical openness to intellectual life.

In 1956 and into early 1957 Graham's plans for New York City represented his most ambitious project yet. As it turned out, the meetings drew tremendous crowds, including one gathering of ninety-two thousand at Yankee Stadium. There were also many life-changing decisions for Christ. But this New York campaign also solidified a decisive break with the past. In New York City, Graham clarified a strategy he had been developing for some time: he would cooperate with whoever would cooperate with him, including mainline Protestants whom other evangelicals considered dangerously liberal. When fundamentalist critics challenged him on this strategy, Graham stood firm.

The result, which many others besides the Billy Graham Evangelistic Association supported, was a clearer distinction between separatist and intentionally narrow fundamentalism and more open, intentionally outgoing evangelicalism. That distinction has not always been recognized by outsiders, but it has been crucial for the history of theologically conservative American Protestants. It draws a straight line from Graham to more recent pastors-communicators-writers such as Bill Hybels, Rick Warren, and Tim Keller. Fundamentalists would seek to protect the gospel by separating from the world, evangelicals would seek to promote it by engaging the world.

Graham was a leader, but he was leading where others were already heading on their own. Soon many were making similar choices: for example, to embrace the musical styles and forms of presentation made ubiquitous by television in place of traditional churchly modes of worship; to exploit aggressively whatever means of mass communication the culture made available; to devise new forms of middle-class church organization and worship that responded to suburban sprawl and the hegemony of the automobile; to learn from the Jesus People about lightening up toward American popular culture; to let charismatic influences move sensibilities in more expressive and therapeutic directions; and to abandon political withdrawal in favor of political involvement.

Unanticipated consequences of these decisions meant that evangelical history did not necessarily move as early leaders expected. As an example, only weeks before *Christianity Today* was launched, Elvis Presley had appeared for the first time on the *Ed Sullivan Show* and had created a sensation that scandalized almost all right-thinking evangelicals and fundamentalists. Few, thus, could have predicted that in many evangelical churches public worship in the early twenty-first century would look and sound more like Elvis Presley on the *Ed Sullivan Show* than the worship at Sunday evening services attended by the evangelicals who were so alarmed by Elvis in 1956. Likewise, few could have foreseen the rise of megachurches attuned to the suburban landscapes created by the interstate highways and the startling expansion of American wealth. Few could have imagined that an appeal to reengage with American public life would lead into culture wars or the transformation of evangelicalism into what some have called "the Republic Party at prayer." Yet what was happening by the mid-1950s paved the way for all of these later developments.

These general evangelical developments also included significant new departures for intellectual life. On many fronts, change was the order of the day. Led by figures such as Carl F. H. Henry, first a handful and then large numbers sought academic credentials from the nation's established research universities that their fundamentalist predecessors had spurned. More generally, rising incomes and social aspirations added evangelicals to the nation's explosive postwar expansion of higher education.

Theologically, more and more evangelicals sought to leave behind the docetic, gnostic, and Manichaean tendencies of historic evangelical theologies—whether the assertive humanism of Charles Finney's revivalism, the social unconcern attending D. L. Moody's evangelism, the prophetic and creationist fixations of premillennial dispensationalism, the intellectual and social passivity of Higher Life spirituality, or the otherworldly preoccupations of some Pentecostals. Disquiet with these elements did not necessarily mean that evangelicals abandoned the foundational commitments that had always propelled their revivals and sustained their communities in ordinary times—including a deep awareness of human sinfulness, a desire to honor Christ, an energetic response to the message of salvation, and a special reliance on the work of the Holy Spirit. But it did mean that more and more evangelicals were coming to feel uneasy about how evangelicals put the mind to use.

But where to go to put that uneasiness to rest? Institutionally there was a problem of limited facilities for expanding interests. Evangelical philanthropy has enjoyed a long and distinguished record, with evangelical levels of giving continuing to measure far above the average through the postwar years and into the present day. But evangelical philanthropy has always focused on the missionary proclamation of the gospel, on immediate relief for pressing human needs, and on local projects attached to local churches. Traditionally, financial support for educational institutions ranked much lower on the agenda, in large part because when evangelicals "lost" the nation's major institutions of higher learning, they lapsed into a practical disillusionment with mainstream higher education. The financial support that their evangelical predecessors had once provided to the nation's leading colleges and universities was provided no more. Fundamentalists and conservative evangelicals did not do what Catholics had tried to do early in their American history, which was to create university-level alternatives to the nation's higher educational establishment. Instead, evangelicals from the late nineteenth century rested content with Bible schools, church-based education, independent theological seminaries, and a corporal's guard of underfunded four-year liberal arts colleges—but no comprehensive universities oriented in principle to first-level intellectual exploration. The result, when in the last decades of the twentieth century numerous evangelicals began to get serious about real learning, was that a number of evangelical colleges and seminaries did exist where scholarship was appreciated, but there were no evangelical institutions with the first-level capacities to compete with the universities where serious intellectual life—however incomplete, partial, or unfriendly to Christianity—was the order of the day.[48]

This situation has begun to change in recent years, but distinctly evangelical institutions of higher learning still possess only a fraction of the financial capacity required to support serious research. In the university endowment league tables for 2005, where a few Catholic institutions show respectable endowments able to support at least some measure of real research—Notre Dame at 18th in the nation, Boston College 41st, Georgetown 78th—Protestant-evangelical institutions do not check in until much lower on the scale—Baylor at 77th, Pepperdine at 115th, Wheaton at 164th, Regent University at 192nd, Messiah at 326th, and Calvin at 395th.[49]

Intellectually there has been perhaps even more uncertainty than institutionally. In recent decades some evangelicals with sectarian roots have become Presbyterians and Episcopalians in the search for worship patterns, theological traditions, and sacramental practices that provide more natural support for intellectual life. But the ongoing toils of the mainline Protestant denominations, especially the genetic inability ever to say no to dominant trends in the nation's elite intellectual culture, have left these denominations unable to provide sharply focused Christian underpinning for Christian learning. A few evangelicals have found sturdier theological resources in conservative Lutheranism, but for

48. A sensitive discussion of this situation is found in Robert Wuthnow, "The Costs of Marginality," a chapter in his book *The Struggle for America's Soul: Evangelicals, Liberals, and Secularism* (Grand Rapids: Eerdmans, 1989), 158–76.

49. 2005 NACUBO Endowment Study (January 30, 2006), www.nacubo.org/prssroom.

a number of reasons related to Lutheran theological and ethnic history, that course of action has not yielded noticeably intellectual results.

More generally, evangelicals who have left the harbors of sectarianism, launched into the sea of contemporary intellectual life, and sought ships ready to run and anchorage during storms have found these things in intellectual affinities more than ecclesiastical fellowships.

Evangelicals have made some of their strongest intellectual moves in philosophy, largely by following the generally neo-Calvinist strategies of Alvin Plantinga and Nicholas Wolterstorff, though only a few have actually joined the Christian Reformed Church that for generations nurtured a proprietary attitude toward formal learning that eventually made it possible for a Plantinga and a Wolterstorff to emerge. Other inspiration for evangelical philosophers is drawn from the virtue ethics of Alasdair MacIntyre or from other Catholic sources, especially going back to Thomas Aquinas and St. Augustine.

The pattern for philosophers has been repeated in other disciplines. Evangelical historians have been encouraged to speak more definitely about the bearing of faith on their subjects by noting how it was earlier done by the Catholic Christopher Dawson, then by George Marsden, who shares much with the neo-Calvinist philosophers, and more recently by the Catholics Eamon Duffy and Brad Gregory. A boomlet in evangelical art history rests squarely on the work of the Dutch Reformed scholar Hans Rookmaaker. Evangelical theology, especially as practiced by a rising generation of eager young scholars, is being pulled along by serious engagement with the Reformed Karl Barth, the Catholic Hans Urs von Balthasar, and the Anglicans Oliver O'Donovan and John Milbank. Evangelical social and political theory is being invigorated by general instruction from the Catholic social tradition and specific teaching of papal encyclicals from Leo XIII's *Rerum Novarum* to John Paul II's *Laborem Exercens* and *Centesimus Annus*. A long-lived and ever-enthusiastic evangelical literary resurgence is almost wholly directed by Catholics (G. K. Chesterton, Walker Percy, Flannery O'Connor, J. R. R. Tolkien) and high-church Anglicans (T. S. Eliot, C. S. Lewis, Dorothy Sayers).

Our editor, Thomas Albert Howard, has made the significant observation that these signs of intellectual vitality among contemporary evangelicals display noteworthy common characteristics. Negatively, they almost never reference the stalwarts that "have defined mainstream evangelicalism—the brothers Wesley, Charles Finney, Billy Graham, Francis Schaeffer, Charles Colson, James Dobson." Neither do they draw obvious inspiration from "revivalist preaching, political activism, dispensational theology, and speculative prophecy." Rather, they have engaged in what Howard calls "selective borrowing" or even "massive pillaging" from "traditions that have historically placed more value on the *vita contemplativa*."[50] They have, in other words, drawn closer to the Protestant traditions that most carefully nurtured Christendom instincts or to Catholicism, which long sustained an entire understanding of Christianity defined by some of the underlying assumptions and ideals of Christendom.

To summarize, American evangelical intellectual life now witnesses a vitality that it had not seen since the nineteenth-century heyday of James Marsh, John Williamson Nevin, Charles Hodge, Joseph Henry, and William G. T. Shedd. But it is a vitality that floats free institutionally and that is

---

50. Thomas Albert Howard, essay review of Duane Litfin, *Conceiving the Christian College*, in *The Cresset* 68 (Trinity 2005): 57–59.

sustained to an unusual degree by theological traditions that evangelicals had long neglected or positively disdained.

Compared to fifty years ago, American evangelicals are more comfortable with the ways of American popular culture, more conscious of the need for intellectual leadership to stand alongside spiritual leadership, more riven by conflicting internal currents, more divided by the influence of energetic but often go-it-alone leaders, more wealthy and thus more able to fund Christian projects outside local churches, and more active politically. In sum, they are more culturally engaged, culturally influenced, intellectually alert, naive, theologically divided, questioning than ever.

In the midst of this upheaval, evangelicals, among many other urgent tasks, are seeking a way forward intellectually.

And here come the Catholics.

If this historical sketch makes any sense, we are now in a position to realize why Catholics and evangelicals are in position to help each other out. Many of the salutary features of Christendom, which provides the cultural sine qua non for sustained and effective learning, have been sustained within American Catholicism. The energizing effects of a personal, often lay-driven revivalism that has always enjoyed an intimate connection with the liberal marketplace of American culture but that can also breathe life into the dry husks of formal Christendom are widely on display in contemporary evangelicalism.

Catholicism possesses several learning-conducive strengths that are weak or underrepresented among evangelicals, most of which are connected to the legacies of Christendom:

* a positive, God-honoring place for matter
* a positive, God-honoring role for reason
* a parish ideal of community (all classes, races, dispositions in one common institution)
* a positive acceptance of history and tradition as gifts from God
* a well-established record of careful legal casuistry
* a long-standing commitment to institutions as capable of connecting present communities with both predecessors and successors

But with these potentially positive legacies of Christendom come also some of its negative aspects. Pietists, evangelicals, and fundamentalists were not simply making things up when they pointed to the damage done to Christianity by spiritual formalism, overweening clericalism, theological liberalism, and political power plays masquerading as religious charisma—that, by the excesses and weaknesses of Christendom. Without going as far as Stanley Hauerwas in his criticism of American mainline Protestantism, it is still possible to agree with Hauerwas that within these bodies the stultifying possibilities of Christendom have in recent decades been more obvious than the ennobling aspects.[51]

For their part, evangelicals possess some learning-conducive strengths that have been weak or underrepresented among Catholics:

* a sharp awareness of how religious formalism and mindless tradition can anesthetize thought

51. For examples of Hauerwas's critique, see (with William H. Willimon) *Resident Aliens* (Nashville: Abingdon, 1981) and *After Christendom* (Nashville: Abingdon, 1991).

* a well-practiced demonstration of the virtue of voluntary organization for mobilizing groups and initiating change

* an insistence on personal engagement, in faith and in learning, as a key to God-honoring personal and group existence

* and above all, the inestimable value (especially in an environment shaped by democratic individualism) of the priesthood of all believers

But naturally enough, evangelical weaknesses with respect to intellectual life have also been manifest for all to see.

The tragedy in 1521 at the Diet of Worms was that both Martin Luther and Johann Eck were correct. Late medieval Catholic Christendom was threatening the gospel and could have led to the evisceration of true Christianity; Protestant individualism harbored the potential to promote spiritual chaos and eventually did lead to weakness in the face of outside cultural forces.

But now, almost five centuries removed from the fateful clash that presaged the division of Western Christian thinking, even as it marked the start of the Reformation, it has become possible for the sharp words exchanged at the Diet of Worms to be read as exhortations for mutual correction rather than as sentences of mutual excommunication, which they were almost universally considered to be from the sixteenth century until, say, January 25, 1959, when at St. Paul's outside the Walls in Rome, Pope John XXIII first announced his intention to convene a new general council of the Catholic Church.

Like the symbol of yin and yang, evangelical and Catholic strengths and weaknesses are aligned with nearly perfect symmetry. It is not, therefore, surprising that all manner of historical reasons exist for Catholics and evangelicals to remain suspicious of each other. There are also, however, compelling theological and intellectual reasons to begin to learn from each other. Why do Catholics need evangelicals? Because evangelicals bring to Christendom personal engagement, personal commitment, and lay mobilization. Why do evangelicals need Catholics? Because Catholics bring to evangelicals many of the time-tested virtues of Christendom.

Allow me to conclude with a prediction. If in the next while Christian learning is to flourish in the United States, that flourishing will likely be led by two kinds of individuals:

Catholics (or older confessional Protestants) who have been touched spiritually by the charismatic movement, by intense personal engagement with the scriptures, or by reconnection to one of Catholicism's own traditions of intense personal devotion, but who, as revived Christian believers, still operate with the assumptions of comprehension, community, proprietorship, and universality of Catholic Christendom at its best.

Or it will come from evangelical Protestants (including Pentecostals) who have come to recognize the docetic, gnostic, and Manichaean tendencies of their evangelical and fundamentalist traditions, who have deliberately repudiated these tendencies while self-consciously embracing the comprehension, community, proprietorship, and universality found in classical Western Christendom, and yet who are still transfixed by the gospel pearl of great price communicated by evangelical traditions and who continue to live in gratitude to the enduring gospel elements of the evangelical tradition.

Without representatives of these two groups—and the two drawing at least some strength and recognition from each other—there seems little future for Christian learning in the American context. With contributions from both sources, things could get interesting, and not only for the intellectual life.[52]

52. I would like to thank Thomas Albert Howard, James Turner, Robert Sullivan, and David Hempton for helpful commentary on an earlier version of this essay.

Enduring Differences, Blurring Boundaries

By James Turner

C hristian learning" marks a huge stretch of territory, even when fenced by "evangelical" and "Catholic." Before setting out to chart even a few of its features, the practical-minded explorer will ask what marks on the landscape would be useful to know. In the eyes of this surveyor at least, three questions loom large. They will guide my search (though not order its findings). First, what might Catholics and evangelicals learn from each other to improve their own practices? Second, how might Catholics and evangelicals cooperate to advance "Christian learning"—if they can even agree on the meaning of such a thing? Third, how might Catholics and evangelicals *together* cooperate with others engaged in higher learning to enrich our common enterprise?

This last inquiry is fundamental. Christian colleges and universities do not function in a void, sealed off from non-Christian counterparts, but operate within the larger ecosystem of American and, increasingly, transnational higher education. Christian institutions of higher learning cannot help but respond to the impulses circulating within that bigger system, even if their responses may be nuanced in distinctive ways. As a result, Christian universities in the United States look a lot more like American state universities than they do like Hungarian or Polish universities, whether Christian or secular. And the higher education network itself forms only one out-of-the-way corner in the vast biosphere of American and, increasingly, globalized economy, society, and culture.

To switch from a biological to an astronomical metaphor might give these musings sharper focus. Evangelical Protestant and Roman Catholic higher learning each form a planet, circling the huge sun of American culture. Other planets revolve in parallel orbits: the flagship state universities; the church-related institutions affiliated with "mainline" Protestant denominations; the elite secular private universities; the historically black schools; the secular liberal-arts colleges; the second-tier state institutions; and so forth. Other solar systems—European, Chinese, South American higher education—may exert a little influence on ours, and vice versa, depending on intellectual proximity, but most of the time such pull is minor compared to local gravitational forces.[53] The biggest sphere in our own system, it is salutary to recall, houses two-year community colleges, while the fastest-growing sphere comprises profit-seeking institutions like the University of Phoenix. Our Copernican trope is inexact, because populations of some planets overlap with others. Xavier University in New Orleans is a historically black Roman Catholic school; the elite, private, and

53. Exceptions to this generalization include the influence of German universities on American higher education through much of the nineteenth century, of Oxford and Cambridge on American liberal-arts colleges from about 1880 to 1930, and of American universities on European ones since the later 1960s.

otherwise secular Emory University retains its Methodist affiliation and its theology faculty. But the metaphor helps us to remember two key facts. Not only does each planet respond to the powerful gravitational pull of the American culture around which it whirls, but the orbit of each planet is also altered by the tug of other planets. We cannot even imagine Christian higher learning, Catholic or evangelical, on its own. And in thinking about its potential accomplishments, we ought to conceive those, at least in part, as contributions to the greater good of the whole system.

Mark Noll and I were asked to aim our telescopes at evangelical Protestant and Roman Catholic higher learning and to report some of the attractions and repulsions they exert on each other and on other orbs in the higher-educational system. Noll planet-gazes from a Protestant evangelical perspective, I from a Roman Catholic point of view. The indefinite article is essential: each of our viewpoints is sui generis, there being no standard-issue evangelical or Catholic angle of vision. Still, each of us does peer through a highly particular lens, even if one of our own manufacture. We can try to correct for the resulting distortions, and certain contingencies help us to do so: Noll has written extensively about all varieties of Christianity, including Catholicism; I have spent most of my historical career studying Protestant and post-Protestant intellectuals. In the end, though, we cannot rise above our fleshly prisons and see directly into the heart of the matters here at hand or any others, and I beg the charitable reader to keep this in mind.

A few other preliminary cautions are in order. Not all evangelicals are Protestant and far from all Catholics are Roman; but in what follows I, like most writers in the United States today, shall use *Catholic* and *evangelical* as shorthand for "Roman Catholic" and "Protestant evangelical."

And I shall intend *evangelical* broadly, to include fellow-traveling scholars like the neo-Calvinists from the Christian Reformed Church's Calvin College. Their deep commitment to a creedal tradition and strong doctrine of the church place them outside stricter and perhaps historically more accurate definitions of American evangelicalism. But this broad nomenclature allows us to get at intellectual alliances and affinities of high importance for our topic that a narrower definition of *evangelical* would elide. The contours of evangelical intellectual and academic life today at least extenuate, perhaps fully justify, this decision. Christian Reformed and like-minded neo-Calvinist scholars are probably overrepresented in the pages of *Books & Culture*, widely understood to be an "evangelical" review. They also received more than their share of fellowships in the Evangelical Scholarship Initiative sponsored by the Pew Charitable Trusts in the 1990s.[54] The Calvin College academic diaspora provides a substantial minority of today's leading self-consciously Christian (Protestant) scholars, and I shall lump the Calvin circle with "real" evangelicals. And why not? A Calvin émigré, Richard Mouw, now presides over America's leading evangelical theological seminary, Fuller.

I shall also deploy another shorthand word, *secular*, in its primary rather than derived meaning.[55] *Secular* did not originally imply *anti*-religious, although people often use the word today with that hostile edge ("secular humanism"). The oldest attested usage of the word (late thirteenth century) actually labeled a type of clergyman—one who lived in "the

---

54. See James Turner, "Something to Be Reckoned With: The Evangelical Mind Awakens," *Commonweal* 126 (January 15, 1999): 11–23, for a discussion of the dynamics of the so-called evangelical intellectual revival (reprinted in James Turner, *Language, Religion, Knowledge: Past and Present* [Notre Dame, IN: University of Notre Dame Press, 2003], chap. 7).

55. *Webster's Third New International Dictionary, Unabridged*, s.v. "secular."

world" rather than in a monastery.[56] *Secular* now first of all means disconnected from religious commitments—related to temporal affairs rather than spiritual—and that is all it will signify in the pages that follow. Evangelical in its early days, Williams College is today secularized, that is, disengaged from any church or faith tradition. But it is not institutionally *hostile* to religious faith or practice. Antireligious institutions do not sponsor an active ecumenical chaplaincy, as Williams does.[57] When, later, we come to discuss characteristic Catholic approaches to intellectual life via universalism and sacramentalism, clarity about the neutral meaning of *secular* will matter a great deal. But *evangelical* and *secular* are not the only slippery terms to figure largely in these pages.

Another is *higher learning,* the precise topic we are charged to address. It can mean "higher education," that is, colleges and universities and the teaching that takes place within them. *Higher learning* can also denote "academic knowledge," that is, erudite discourses grounded in specialized bodies of information. Nowadays academic knowledge is most often produced and consumed within institutions of higher education, though not always. *Higher learning* thus gives us a very capacious blanket. It covers both the inculcation of knowledge and the advancement of knowledge—that is, teaching and research—as well as the institutions in which both endeavors usually take place. So if we are to reflect seriously on "the future of Christian learning," we have to address at least three broad areas of inquiry: institutional structures, pedagogy, and research. More precisely, we need to ask about (1) potential points of contact and cooperation between evangelical and Catholic colleges and universities, (2) Catholic and evangelical practices of teaching, and (3)

56. *Oxford English Dictionary*, s.v. "secular."
57. http://www.williams.edu/Chaplain/.

distinctive features of Catholic and evangelical academic research.

The first of these issues can be dealt with fairly briefly, for there is little chance today of significant institutional interaction between evangelical and Catholic colleges and universities. This assessment may seem bleakly abrupt; but it is, for better or worse, realistic. There are two reasons that these ships will almost certainly continue to pass in the night.

The first is that evangelicals and Catholics conceive very differently what it means to be a Christian college or university. With few exceptions, Catholic schools have shed the ghetto mentality that strongly marked American Catholicism before 1960. Most of them now whirl in a complicated dance with mainstream secular higher education. These Catholic colleges and universities hope to preserve a distinctively Catholic character while fully integrating into American academe.[58] The indefinite article before "character" is apt because the content of "Catholic character" varies from school to school, depending on history, present orientation, and, very commonly, founding religious order. "Jesuit" carries different freight than "Dominican." Some commentators (usually but not always theologically conservative) consider this ambition to swim in the mainstream badly misguided. These critics believe that adopting the same

58. Some characteristic explorations are Theodore M. Hesburgh, CSC, ed., *The Challenge and Promise of a Catholic University* (Notre Dame, IN: University of Notre Dame Press, 1994); Michael J. Buckley, SJ, *The Catholic University as Promise and Project: Reflections in a Jesuit Idiom* (Washington, DC: Georgetown University Press, 1998); and Mark W. Roche, *The Intellectual Appeal of Catholicism and the Idea of a Catholic University* (Notre Dame, IN: University of Notre Dame Press, 2003).

academic criteria and aims as Harvard University or Kansas University inevitably means setting foot on a slippery slope sliding straight into secularity.[59] But such skeptics constitute only a small (if eloquently outspoken) minority among leaders of American Catholic higher education. The majority believe Catholic universities can compete successfully on the same academic playing field as Duke and Texas without losing their (Catholic) souls. Maybe this optimism ultimately flows from the Catholic stress on the universality of human reason, maybe from Catholic sacramentalism—about both of which more later. In any case, most Catholic schools not only happen to have but *welcome* a substantial admixture of non-Catholics, non-Christians, and nonbelievers in their faculties and student bodies.

Most evangelical schools, in contrast, conceive of a Christian college as of Christians, by Christians, and for Christians. These colleges typically require at least their permanent faculty to adhere to some rule of faith. In fact, the Council for Christian Colleges and Universities (CCCU), the principal association of evangelical institutions, accepts as full members solely schools that "hire as full-time faculty members and administrators only persons who profess faith in Jesus Christ."[60] There is nothing unreasonable about this stipulation, any more than it is unreasonable to oblige the president of the United States to swear to uphold the Constitution. But such a precept implies a very dissimilar

---

59. E.g., Alasdair MacIntyre, "Catholic Universities: Dangers, Hopes, Choices," in *Higher Learning and Catholic Traditions*, ed. Robert E. Sullivan (Notre Dame, IN: University of Notre Dame Press, 2001); James Tunstead Burtchaell, CSC, *The Dying of the Light: The Disengagement of Colleges and Universities from Their Christian Churches* (Grand Rapids: Eerdmans, 1998). Burtchaell's indictment covers Protestant as well as Catholic institutions; the point here is that he is writing as a Catholic critic, including Catholic institutions in his critique.

60. http://www.cccu.org/about/contentID.5&ChildContentID=7/ns_about .asp.

conception of university or college from the norm in Catholic higher education. No Catholic institution is a full member of the CCCU, and the only Catholic college even on the long list of CCCU *affiliates* is the Franciscan University of Steubenville. Steubenville is one of a handful of conservative or traditionalist or orthodox—choose your term: they are all loaded—institutions that stand proudly and even defiantly athwart the mainstream of American Catholic higher education: a stream they think polluted by secular liberalism and half-hearted Catholicism.[61] If one went looking within the universe of evangelical higher education for a structural (*not* theological or ideological) analogue to the Franciscan University of Steubenville, the parallel would be a school like Bob Jones University: likewise proudly purist and boldly separatist, positioned purposefully on the hyper-conservative margin. That only Steubenville, of all Catholic schools, chooses to link itself with the CCCU suggests the gulf in self-conception between conventional Catholic institutions of higher education and their counterparts in the evangelical mainstream.

Indeed, the commonplace rhetoric of evangelical higher education implies that most Catholic institutions, with their open-door policies, do not even qualify as Christian. Consider the name of that association of which Steubenville is the only Catholic affiliate. I have admired the work of the

61. http://www.cccu.org/about/ns_affiliates.asp; http://www.franciscan.edu/home2/Content/main.aspx. Franciscan University of Steubenville is unusual among even the handful of very conservative Catholic institutions because of its leaning toward the charismatic movement within the Catholic church—a consequence of the long presidency of Rev. Michael Scanlan, TOR, a man who is evidently also charismatic in the Weberian sense. For a recent assessment of this complex institution from a "leftish" Catholic viewpoint, see John L. Allen, "What Kind of Model is Steubenville?" *National Catholic Reporter*, February 11, 2000, available at http://www.highbeam.com/library/docFree.asp?DOCID=1G1:59607728.

Council for Christian Colleges and Universities since coming to know the organization many years ago when it was still the Christian College Coalition. I have admired its work but often regretted its language, which used routinely to imply that nonmember colleges were somehow not Christian or not fully Christian, whatever they claimed. The CCCU website still refers, in what seems to outsiders a demeaning tone, to merely "religiously affiliated" institutions in contrast to the organization's own "intentionally Christ-centered institutions." Some of these "religiously affiliated" but nonevangelical Christian colleges and universities, working from different theological presuppositions, may be forgiven for believing that they have a right to understand "intentionally Christ-centered" in their own ways—and may wonder how evangelical schools received a monopoly on discerning what Christianity implies for higher learning. Possibly such exclusivist language stems from contemporary evangelicalism's origin in the purist, separatist fundamentalism of the early twentieth century.[62] Perhaps now mostly formulaic, such rhetoric nonetheless grates on the sensibilities of other Christians in higher education. More to the point here, its embodiment in the missions of evangelical colleges stands radically at odds with the characteristic approach of Catholic institutions. It is hard to imagine their respective presidents, provosts, and deans collaborating on a regular, ongoing basis.

But there is a second, upsetting, but intensely practical obstacle to evangelical-Catholic institutional cooperation. "It's a jungle out there" is, unfortunately, a catchphrase that applies as much to the institutional behavior of colleges

62. See Joel A. Carpenter, *Revive Us Again: The Reawakening of American Fundamentalism* (New York: Oxford University Press, 1997), and George M. Marsden, *Reforming Fundamentalism: Fuller Seminary and the New Evangelicalism* (Grand Rapids: Eerdmans, 1987).

as to the conduct of business corporations. The notorious *U.S. News* rankings are only the most storied gauge of success in the struggle in which each school strives to clamber over its peers and to attract better-prepared students, more tuition dollars, more alumni donations, more faculty fellowships. And within the peculiarly savage Darwinian ecology of American higher education—what we might call, echoing Tennyson, education "red in tooth and claw/with ravine"—the leading Catholic universities occupy a niche isolated from the niche occupied by the best evangelical schools. Notre Dame, Georgetown, and Boston College aspire to parity with major private universities. Notre Dame and Georgetown have cracked the top 25 in the *U.S. News* ranking; Boston College would love to get there. An academically ambitious evangelical university, if allowing non-Christians on its faculty, might model itself in some ways on Notre Dame: Baylor University's aspirations are sometimes described as becoming a "Protestant Notre Dame." But Notre Dame is not going to hook up in any substantial way with Baylor, for the same reason that Baylor is not going to hitch its star to Mercer University, even though Mercer is likewise self-consciously "founded on Baptist traditions and principles."[63] Baylor and Notre Dame are both looking in the opposite direction: *above* their current echelon in the academic rating game.

This dynamic is hardly appetizing, but it is a fact of intercollegiate life today, and it plays out in similar ways up and down the higher-educational ladder. Colleges and universities that see themselves as approximate peers in academic mission or in academic strength can and do usefully work together. The Consortium for Institutional Cooperation (CIC)

63. http://www2.mercer.edu/BSF/About/default.htm.

built around the Big Ten universities[64] offers an excellent example—as does the CCCU. On quite specific, practical matters where there is nothing to lose, like joining library consortia, even big rats and little mice will collaborate: but not when a hefty chunk of cheese is at stake. Less cynically, one could argue that the largest interests of Christian learning demand that Notre Dame strive to become a Catholic Harvard or Michigan and that it will not get there by swimming with smaller fry. Notre Dame does not even club with other Catholic universities, except in superficial ways. In the feeding frenzy of intercollegiate competition for status, differences in standing and vision will preclude continuing, extensive cooperation between Boston College and its near neighbor Gordon College or between Notre Dame and its near neighbors Goshen College, Wheaton College, and Calvin College.

Yet many individual professors at schools such as Boston College and Notre Dame deeply admire the work of peers at places like Gordon, Goshen, Wheaton, and Calvin. And while Notre Dame may prefer to rub shoulders with Duke and Princeton rather than Calvin and Gordon, it does not hesitate to cherry-pick top scholars from its evangelical neighbors—recently, my coauthor Mark Noll. Individual-level interactions, it seems to me, are where operative alliances between evangelicals and Catholics in higher education have been and will continue to be formed: through personal, not institutional, association. Connections professors make, and examples they set for each other, will link individual faculty members (or small groups of professors), not presidents and provosts; and such ties will concern teaching and especially research, not institutional teamwork. In the classroom and

64. The CIC also includes the University of Chicago and the University of Illinois at Chicago.

even more often in the scholarly journals is where Catholic and evangelical academics find common ground—and where they might also identify useful differences, in order to learn from each other.

Let us then forget about trying to find the road to utopia and turn instead to the real world of teaching and research. Teaching and research are mutually supporting but differently oriented activities. To ask how Catholics might do each differently from evangelicals—or do each *like* evangelicals but differently from *other* academics—is really to pose two distinct, although overlapping problems. So in the pages that follow teaching and research will be approached separately.

Let us take teaching first. Here I wish to reflect on pedagogy at three different levels: in the classroom, in curricular development, and in extracurricular aspirations. The disciplinary substance of teaching can wait until we consider research, since such substance comes from research. To illustrate: It is hard to imagine (although not quite impossible) that a Christian historian could profess in the classroom a consistent classical Marxism-Leninism, presuming materialist determinism. But the historian's repugnance is only derivatively a question of classroom practices; it is primarily a matter of how Christian axioms shape the construction of knowledge in the field of history—that is, an issue concerning research. For now, instead, we shall examine not what one teaches but how one teaches.

How, then, do evangelicals and Catholics teach? Do their faith traditions and religious practices shape their work in the seminar room, lecture hall, art studio, Chemistry 101 lab? If so, do evangelical and Catholic college and university teachers act very differently, or do they share common behaviors? How do both groups compare to teachers at similar but secular institutions? Frankly, no one knows. The foregoing questions are all empirical ones. To answer them requires data, and systematically gathered data do not exist. There is only a little anecdotal evidence, to be culled from prescriptive books written about teaching from a Christian perspective—most of them written, so far as I know, by Protestants.[65] These works lead one to believe that good teaching by a Christian looks like good teaching by a non-Christian, with the differences lying in motivation and self-conception rather than actual practices. But this conclusion is extremely fragile in the present state of knowledge. Any educational researcher interested in college classroom practices has a research agenda ready and waiting.

Until such research is done, all one can honestly say about Catholic approaches to teaching, in implicit or explicit comparison with evangelical approaches, amounts to more or less idiosyncratic speculation. That severe limitation being understood, we can go on to ask how evangelical and Catholic faith traditions and religious sensibilities *might* influence teaching. Two main possibilities strike me. The first lies in conceptions of the college's role in the formation of students, the second in the structure of the curriculum as a whole.

Christianity practically demands that teachers regard education as the holistic formation of students as moral as well

---

65. E.g., among recent works, Richard T. Hughes, *The Vocation of a Christian Scholar: How Christian Faith Can Sustain the Life of the Mind* (Grand Rapids: Eerdmans, 2005); Mark R. Schwehn, *Exiles from Eden: Religion and the Academic Vocation in America* (New York: Oxford University Press, 1993); and compare Mark R. Schwehn, ed., *Everyone a Teacher* (Notre Dame, IN: University of Notre Dame Press, 2000); and "Religious Perspectives and Teaching: Reflections on Practice," pt. 3 of *Religion, Scholarship, and Higher Education: Perspectives, Models, and Future Prospects,* ed. Andrea Sterk (Notre Dame, IN: University of Notre Dame Press, 2002).

as intellectual persons. Within the structure and ideology of American higher education at large, this obligation extends primarily to undergraduate students: graduate students are understood as already shaped adults, in need principally of professional formation (which, to be sure, has its own moral dimensions). This conception of undergraduate teaching as holistic personal formation is far from exclusively Christian or even exclusively religious. Many secular liberal-arts colleges—granted, usually of Christian origin—still understand their purpose as helping students to shape themselves into well-integrated persons of moral seriousness. Carleton College in Minnesota, an ex-Congregationalist institution, offers one example.[66] And to judge from the percentage of Carleton's alumni who devote a year or two after graduation to volunteering for Habitat for Humanity or in inner-city schools, it appears that the college does a fine job. But probably—a judgment based only on personal experience[67]—this particular sense of educational mission, as holistic formation of moral persons, is more nearly generic among Christian colleges than among secular ones, especially when the observer shifts her gaze from free-standing liberal-arts colleges of Protestant origin, like Carleton, to undergraduate colleges housed in large universities, particularly state universities.

And Christian colleges usually go a large step beyond *moral* formation: they aspire to formation in faith. This latter striving may face greater complications at Catholic than evangelical institutions. A big part of the Catholic-college problem stems from religious demographics. Catholic colleges and universities typically house a substantial fraction of

66. I happen to know of this aspect of a Carleton education because my younger son was graduated there.

67. Especially experience in the Lilly Seminar on Religion and Higher Education between 1996 and 1999, for an overview of which see Sterk, ed., *Religion, Scholarship, and Higher Education.*

non-Catholic students—less than 20 percent at Notre Dame, but 30 percent at Boston College and almost half at Georgetown. At DePaul, the nation's largest Catholic university, 70 percent of the student body is not Catholic.[68] And many faculty are not Catholic: nearly half at Notre Dame, probably a majority at Boston College, Georgetown, and DePaul. Among the non-Catholic faculty, a substantial number are not Christian. Notre Dame struggles to keep a majority of its faculty Catholic; most Catholic colleges and universities seem not to fret as much about this issue. Three of the four universities mentioned above require every undergraduate to take a pair of theology courses, but that requirement cannot accomplish a great deal in the face of such religious diversity.[69] A dose of theology may give a Baptist or agnostic student a better-informed notion of Catholicism. It will not go far toward forming her in her own faith, or any other.

Yet even if 100 percent of students and faculty at a college were Catholic, Catholics would still approach formation in faith differently from evangelicals. Catholics inherit a strongly hierarchical and liturgical religious tradition. Its hierarchical aspect includes a history of privileging priests (and others in vowed religious life) over laity. The exaltation of clergy has lessened since the Second Vatican Council (1962–65), but its consequences persist. Through its long past, the Catholic church fostered multifaceted and powerful thinking about the religious formation of priests, nuns, monks, and religious brothers, but comparatively little reflection on the formation of lay men and women—and much of that little modeled on

68. Data from the universities' websites. I cite Notre Dame, Georgetown, and Boston College as academically the most highly ranked Catholic universities.

69. DePaul replaced the theology requirement with a religious-studies requirement in its liberal-arts curriculum (http://arc.depaul.edu/pdf/bulletin/UGRD_LAS_Aut2006.pdf, p. 8. This is perhaps understandable given the low proportion of Catholics among its students.

clerical formation. (It is only fair to add that the tradition includes devotional works like Thomas à Kempis's *Imitation of Christ*, which, though originally meant for monks, transcends the clerical-lay distinction—as a great many Protestants have discovered.) In addition to this paucity of attention to lay formation, nonclerical faculty members at Catholic schools seem rarely to talk to students about faith (or such is my observation)—perhaps even at a subconscious level they half-believe it inappropriate to do so. Such conversations were traditionally what priests undertook, after all, not laypeople. Insofar as they aspire to faith formation, then, Catholic colleges have something to learn from the practices of other Christian traditions, including notably evangelicalism. Anecdotal evidence suggests that religiously serious younger Catholic academics do sometimes behave in everyday religious self-expression more like evangelicals than like their older Catholic colleagues. The possibility would be worth study.

The liturgical aspect of the Catholic tradition stresses participation in ancient, diverse, and richly evolved rituals, most notably of course the sacrifice (as Catholics understand it) of the Mass. To take part in the Triduum—the services commemorating Holy Thursday, Good Friday, and the Easter vigil—at Notre Dame's Basilica of the Sacred Heart is a deeply moving religious and aesthetic experience, and the aesthetic cannot be easily separated from the religious. Such ritual experience is a strength of faith formation in Catholic colleges. In ritual, the cognitive, emotional, physical, and aesthetic dimensions of human nature merge seamlessly in a single spiritual encounter: an experience lived by a participant not as an isolated unit but as an integral part of a worshiping community. Ritual speaks to the whole human person as a member of a group united in common orientation toward the divine. And that is how normal people live: as whole human persons in communities. Even the most antiliturgical Protestants have their rituals (even if they may shy away from the word), but ritual is especially rich in Catholicism and central to Catholic religious practice, including the routines in colleges and universities. Boston College's website brags that Mass is celebrated on its campus seventy-seven times a week.[70] Any big Catholic school could make a similar boast. But ritual celebration in community—though often an intense experience, at a deeply personal level—does not alone develop in students a mature, individual, personal appropriation of their faith.

For this attainment, smaller-scale, even person-to-person encounters may be required. Evangelicals historically have almost specialized in developing such face-to-face contexts for sharing faith. In recent decades campus ministries at Catholic colleges have widely undertaken their own initiatives of this sort—in some cases, though by no means all, probably drawing self-consciously on the evangelical example. For example, universities as different as DePaul, Notre Dame, Loyola Marymount, and St. Thomas (Minnesota) now sponsor small, voluntary, often nondenominational groups that meet to study the Bible or otherwise to "pray, reflect, and discuss issues of life and faith."[71] Parallel community-service programs—an activity with a longer and stronger tradition in Catholic higher education— encourage students to express their faith in helping people in need. Service programs extend beyond the undergraduate years and can explicitly integrate service with faith formation. The Jesuit Volunteer Corps annually sends some three

70. http://www.bc.edu/bc_org/rvp/pubaf/chronicle/v13/o21/masses.html.
71. Quotation from Loyola Marymount University's campus ministry website (http://ministry.lmu.edu/clc/index.htm).

hundred members (most of them recent Catholic college graduates) to work for a year with people "marginalized by society" while living with other volunteers "in apostolic community."[72] Similarly, Notre Dame's Alliance for Catholic Education sustains some thirty houses across the American South and Southwest where five or six recent graduates (most but not all from Notre Dame) share spiritual and community life while teaching in impoverished parochial schools.[73] Such creative efforts to ground faith formation in small, intentional groups closely resemble similar initiatives at evangelical colleges, such as the Discipleship Small Group Ministry at Wheaton, the "bread groups" at Gordon, or the "discipleship groups" at Biola.[74] As a result, Catholic colleges and universities—in this respect—now more closely resemble their evangelical cousins than ever before.

Through the first two-thirds of the twentieth century, Catholic colleges probably did a better job of *intellectual* than *spiritual* formation in faith. However, the once-heavy curricular requirements inculcating Catholic intellectual traditions fell away in the wake of Vatican II and the subsequent convergence of Catholic higher education with standard American models. As mentioned above, one or two required theology courses are still commonplace—though, judging from college catalogs, these often appear too erratic in content to do much to form intellectually competent Catholics. For the most part, intellectual faith

72. https://www.jesuitvolunteers.org/default.cfm/PID=1.25.

73. https://ace.nd.edu/ace/index.cfm; Michael Pressley, ed., *Teaching Service and Alternative Teacher Education: Notre Dame's Alliance for Catholic Education* (Notre Dame, IN: University of Notre Dame Press, 2002). The young teachers receive a summer's intensive preparation in pedagogy at Notre Dame before going off to their assignments, then return to campus for a second summer's work, with an MEd awarded for this academic training.

74. See respective websites.

formation has become a matter of student choice. So-called Catholic Studies programs are proliferating in Catholic universities; as of 2003 there were around thirty of these nationwide.[75] Catholic Studies programs are typically undergraduate majors or minors (although at least one MA program exists, at the University of St. Thomas in Minnesota) that integrate Catholic literature, art, philosophy, and theology. Some curricula have a specific focus, such as Notre Dame's minor ("concentration") in Catholic Social Tradition; others are more broadly integrative, like the first and still largest program, at St. Thomas. Given the rich intellectual and aesthetic traditions of Catholicism, these programs have a lot to draw on—more than American evangelical intellectual traditions offer, as Mark Noll has "scandalously" argued.[76] In this respect, Catholic higher education has something to offer evangelicals in return for what it may have learned from evangelicals about methods of spiritual formation.

This brings us to the second main point about teaching: the character of the curriculum as a whole. Catholics and evangelicals—and many other people—believe that the world around us, in all its complex variety, is the creation of one Supreme Being. It seems to follow from this axiom (or so most intellectually minded Christians, Jews, and Muslims historically have believed) that all knowledge forms a seamless whole—in principle—because all knowledge refers either to the one Creator or to that Creator's single creation. "In principle" provides a necessary

75. http://consortium.villanova.edu/resources/cathstudies/zroster.htm.

76. Mark A. Noll, *The Scandal of the Evangelical Mind* (Grand Rapids: Eerdmans, 1994). Cf. Hughes, *Vocation of a Christian Scholar*, 43–44; "Are Evangelicals Impacting Education, and Vice Versa [interview with Nathan O. Hatch]," *Reformed Quarterly* 16 (Spring 1997), available at http://www.rts.edu/quarterly/spring97/qa.html.

qualification: fallible human beings will inevitably fail to see all the connections.

It would seem, in any case, that the curriculum in a Christian college ought to ground itself in this immediately relevant implication of Christian faith. The structure of the curriculum, that is, should help students to recognize the unity of knowledge, reflecting the unity of creation. In fact, through most of the nineteenth century almost all Protestant colleges in the United States offered a senior course, called Moral Philosophy or Moral Science, that did exactly this.[77] The course—proceeding from theological first principles to the various specific fields of knowledge—gave, as one student remembered, "a bird's-eye view of human knowledge, effort, and affectivity."[78] A modern reader can recover some sense of the course's breadth by recalling that the present array of university social-science departments, plus the philosophy department, hived off from moral philosophy in the late nineteenth century.

Before the later 1960s Catholic colleges tried to do the same sort of thing in a different way, by prescribing for students a huge quantity of neoscholastic philosophy—a dose so massive that Catholic undergraduates had, in effect, two majors: philosophy and whatever discipline they longingly declared that they really wanted to study.[79] (One conse-

77. Wilson Smith, *Professors and Public Ethics: Studies of Northern Moral Philosophers before the Civil War* (Ithaca, NY: Cornell University Press, 1956); Daniel Walker Howe, *The Unitarian Conscience: Harvard Moral Philosophy, 1805–1861* (Cambridge, MA: Harvard University Press, 1970); and Donald H. Meyer, *The Instructed Conscience: The Shaping of the American National Ethic* (Philadelphia: University of Pennsylvania Press, 1972). The best-selling example was Francis Wayland, *The Elements of Moral Science*, ed. Joseph L. Blau (1837; Cambridge, MA: Belknap Press, 1963).

78. G. Stanley Hall, *Life and Confessions of a Psychologist* (New York: D. Appleton, 1923), 168. Hall was recalling President Mark Hopkins's course at Williams College.

79. Gleason, *Contending with Modernity*.

quence: Catholic colleges housed the majority of philosophy teachers in the United States through the first two-thirds of the twentieth century. One of my philosophical colleagues impishly says that the regnant "American philosophy" of the era of William James and John Dewey was not pragmatism but neo-Thomism!) The requirement at many Catholic colleges today that students take a couple of philosophy courses is a faint echo of this past.

The echo is very faint, and not just at Catholic schools. Catholic education has pretty well given up any serious attempt to demonstrate and exemplify the unity of knowledge. To the best of my limited awareness, so have evangelical colleges. At least, some time spent trolling through programmatic information available online indicates that enthusiasm to display the unity of knowledge at evangelical schools is almost entirely confined to mission statements and similar documents.

Why did Christian colleges—Catholic and Protestant alike—abdicate this project of building a curriculum around, or at least congruent with, Christian principles of knowledge? The renunciation, I would argue, was more or less forced on them by the rise of disciplinary specialization in the decades around 1900. Specialization had always formed a necessary precondition for the advance of learning: no researcher can cover every subject. But *disciplinary* specialization was a new thing in the nineteenth century. Disciplinary specialization required the subdivision of knowledge into specialized domains ("disciplines," in a new sense of that old word) that were *methodologically* inaccessible to workers in other such specialized domains. As late as the 1890s a single scholar might write and teach authoritatively—and on the basis of genuine specialized expertise—about medieval architecture, English Renaissance poetry, Dante, and the reconstruction of the temple of Zeus at Olympia (Charles Eliot Norton did so).[80] By 1920 such intellectual range smacked of dilettantism and offended the canons of scholarship. The emergence of these new scholarly norms reflected the fraying of ties between Christianity (with its universalist, integrating assumptions) and academic knowledge, though dechristianization was far from the only reason that disciplinary specialization developed.[81]

We now teach in the splintered aftermath of this restructuring of learning. Knowledge lies scattered around us in great, unconnected pieces, like lonely mesas jutting up in the northeastern Arizona desert. Today it is difficult, if not impossible, for a molecular biologist to read with full comprehension the professional publications of a cognitive psychologist, or vice versa, or for a layperson to read either's.[82] Even if one believes molecular biology and cognitive psychology to be studying facets of a single creation, how in the world could one trace the path that leads from one to the other in the present organization of knowledge? If Catholic and evangelical academics wish seriously to wrestle with this quandary, they will find themselves in the same ring, grappling with the same adversary.

Many evangelicals and Catholics do seem increasingly to accept the need to work together. In academic life today, one often finds evangelical and Catholic professors working with a sense of common purpose in the endeavor to develop a proper place for religious commitments in intellectual life.

80. James Turner, *The Liberal Education of Charles Eliot Norton* (Baltimore: Johns Hopkins University Press, 1999).

81. For a fuller account, see Jon H. Roberts and James Turner, *The Sacred and the Secular University* (Princeton, NJ: Princeton University Press, 2000), chap. 5.

82. The preceding three sentences are adapted from Turner, *Language, Religion, Knowledge*, 133.

Disciplinary associations founded by evangelicals—the Society of Christian Philosophers, Christians in Political Science, *ACE!* the Conference on Faith and History—now attract Catholic members, even have Catholic officers. Catholics write for the evangelical intellectual review *Books & Culture*. Notre Dame, meanwhile, has attracted such important evangelical scholars as George Marsden, Mark Noll, and Alvin Plantinga and has become a magnet for evangelical graduate students in certain fields, notably philosophy, sociology, and history. The four evangelical historians currently working on one of the CCCU's networking grants to Christian scholars include a recent Notre Dame PhD and a Notre Dame graduate student.[83] Such cooperation across once bitter divides makes it possible to contemplate rebuilding a generically Christian, unified framework of knowledge with practical effect in the curriculum—a framework that might even appeal, in modified form, to non-Christians.

And Catholic academics may have a distinctive contribution to make to this common task. Traditionally, the great strength of Catholic intellectual life has been just that: tradition.[84] That is, Roman Catholics, much more often than twentieth-century evangelicals, heard their own voices as participants in a long-standing and multisided conversation stretching back continuously over more than two millennia. During the later nineteenth century, with the papacy under siege and the Vatican set against modernity, this respect for intellectual tradition jelled into an artificially rigid, sometimes factitious neo-Thomism. This revived Thomism—becoming increasingly subtle, increasingly faithful to Aquinas—remained the center of gravity of Catholic intellectual

83. A project directed by Professor Stephen G. Alter of Gordon College.
84. This and the following paragraph are adapted from Turner, *Language, Religion, Knowledge*, 133–34.

life until the mid-twentieth century. Whatever its defects, neo-Thomism kept alive among Catholics, even deepened, their powerful sense that intellectual life *meant* thinking within a tradition. Up to the 1960s at least, Catholic writers were as likely to interrogate Aristotle or Anselm or Aquinas as their own contemporaries. When the Second Vatican Council's spirit of *aggiornamento* opened the church's windows to the contemporary world, the winds of change sometimes drowned out these voices of the past.

But never entirely, and many Catholic intellectuals soon recovered their sense of the gravity of tradition. Roman Catholics are far from the only Christians with a strong investment in intellectual tradition. Notably for our purposes, Christian Reformed and Anglican intellectuals share this proclivity and have, as a result, made hefty contributions to enriching evangelical intellectual life. But as the evangelical scholar of religion Richard Hughes writes, "the Catholic intellectual heritage" offers "a stunning array of intellectual resources to which, in fact, no other Christian tradition in the Western world can compare."[85] And tradition matters if college teachers are ever to resolve the problem of the fragmentation of knowledge. For only within an ongoing framework of shared questions and axioms, rooted in shared texts, can inquirers find common ground even for coherent disagreement, much less mutual engagement. The most intellectually productive traditions are apt to be loose-jointed, encouraging experiment rather than conformity: rife with disputation, disagreement, development, divergence. If designers of college curricula are ever to reestablish communication among the scattered realms of learning, ever to find a collective ground of discourse, ever, in short, to give voice again to the silenced unity of knowledge, they will do

85. Hughes, *Vocation of a Christian Scholar*, 43–44.

so only by thinking in terms of a new intellectual tradition that evangelicals and Catholics alike can share. And that tradition must also be comprehensible and appealing to non-Christians and nonbelievers, even if they cannot accept its most fundamental axiom, the God of all creation. No one today can conceive what such a tradition might look like, though it is hard to imagine that it would be so exclusively European or so overwhelmingly male as the traditions we have grown out of.

A curriculum built around, or grounded in, such a tradition would not have to violate the integrity of the present individual disciplines in order to help students think about their studies in broader, more interconnected ways. Courses exploring the foundations and interconnections of disciplines, for instance, could infuse teaching with wider meanings and resonance, as the old moral philosophy course did for a different age with different structures of knowledge. The doctrine of creation gives Christians (and Jews and Muslims) a particularly strong motive to work toward such curricular renovation.[86] But one does not have to trust in one of the Abrahamic faiths to believe that all knowledge ought somehow to hang together; to lament its present division; to hope for its reconnection.[87] There is modest reason to think, therefore, that Christian colleges and universities may have a not-so-modest contribution to make to higher education at large.

86. Religiously serious Muslims and Jews would have the same motivation but do not have, in the United States, the same opportunity: a vast array of institutions of higher education.

87. Edward O. Wilson, *Consilience: The Unity of Knowledge* (New York: Alfred A. Knopf, 1998), argues this hope from distinctly non-Abrahamic axioms. It is an interesting and revealing exercise to ask whether an integrative curriculum constructed along "Wilsonian" lines but stripped of Wilson's materialist determinism would be compatible with a similar curriculum constructed along Christian lines but stripped of explicit theism. I judge probably not but could be wrong.

What if, in fact, evangelicals are starting to pay serious attention to Catholic and other chronologically deep and intellectually complex Christian intellectual traditions? What if younger Catholic professors and Catholic campus ministries are behaving more like evangelicals in their efforts to aid students in developing a mature faith? Then, perhaps, Catholic and evangelical approaches to teaching are converging. How far might such a trend go? Might it even influence pedagogy outside of self-consciously Christian colleges? Answers to such questions are anybody's guess. Catholic and evangelical faith traditions are very different in character. That reality alone surely poses formidable obstacles to eradicating deep disparities between Catholic and evangelical colleges. And, as far as influencing secular planets in our educational solar system, Christian commitment itself may turn some non-Christians away from anything originating in it. All one can responsibly conclude is that change is in the air and the future of Christian higher education is open ended.

A similarly fluid situation exists today in the final area of "higher learning": research. This volatility stems, in part, from changing attitudes over the last couple of decades toward religiously grounded or religiously motivated research: a decidedly encouraging shift for what evangelicals commonly call "Christian scholars." (Catholics less often use the distinguishing label, even when self-consciously working from Christian presuppositions, for reasons that will become clear below.) I see two principal causes for the development of this more favorable climate. The first is the substantial contributions to scholarship made in some fields by scholars working from an explicitly Christian point of view. For instance, in the last generation a band of evangelical historians of religion (including notably my coauthor Mark Noll), who are not shy about professing the impact of Christianity on their work, have altered how American historians at large understand the place of religion in our country's past. To cite an example from a different academic sphere, two philosophers writing in complex and dissimilar ways out of Catholic backgrounds have emerged among the leading voices of North American philosophy: Charles Taylor and Alasdair MacIntyre. The influence of such scholars outside Christian circles has started to unsettle the long regnant axiom that religious belief has nothing to do with research, that mixing the two even violates the integrity of research. A scholar might disagree sharply with Noll or MacIntyre, but no one can plausibly say that, in these instances, Christianity has added nothing to learning.

The second chief reason for a new openness in some academic circles to religiously oriented scholarship is the resurgence of religion as a force in the post–cold war world. The removal of Soviet-American rivalry as the straitjacket of geopolitics (and geopolitical analysis) has made clear the enduring vitality and power of religious faith in many parts of the globe. No serious observer can any longer cling to the old, rather smug conviction that modernization will gradually make religion fade away (even if the observer still wishes it would). The assumption that faith is a waning force, a theory inherited from Victorian agnostics and once widely shared among European and American academics, is now seen to be patently wrong as a matter of practical fact—indeed dangerously wrong in today's world. In consequence, scholars who are themselves secular in outlook are taking more interest in religion as a living force. And especially against the background of Islamicist radicalism, ultra-Orthodox Israeli nationalism, and weird Christian sects

Many economists would sadly disagree.—

like the Branch Davidians, ordinary Christianity no longer seems so musty and atavistic. Christianity is certainly not chic in many academic circles, but neither can it be consigned to irrelevance.

Christian scholars do not travel in a single rut, and noteworthy differences distinguish Catholic and evangelical approaches to "Christian scholarship." In the pages that remain, I shall sketch my understanding of these differences and their consequences: a perception shaped by peculiar personal experience. For six years I directed an organization *Hmm.* called the Erasmus Institute. Its remit was to bring the diverse intellectual traditions of the Abrahamic faiths, especially Christianity, to bear on nontheological research and scholarship in the humanities and social sciences. Among other programs, the Erasmus Institute annually offered ten residential fellowships at Notre Dame, allowing scholars to pursue individual research projects falling within the broad aims of the institute. The great majority of these Erasmus Fellows hailed from four fields: history, literature, philosophy, and political theory. The institute never meant to focus on these particular disciplines—in fact, the staff beat the bushes to scare up applicants from others—but scholars from these four domains applied for and won almost all the fellowships. This bald fact may itself indicate which disciplines today offer the greatest possibilities for scholarship informed by Christian intellectual traditions: not the warmest hospitality but the most openings for promising research.

When one bumps into scholars every day for the nine months of the academic year, one learns something of their work. Stereotypes aside, the genus *philosophiæ doctor* is reasonably social. Even the rare hermit crabs among the Erasmus Fellows scurried weekly out of their offices for the fellows' seminar. So I was able to compare, year after year, approaches to research of Catholic scholars, evangelical scholars, and (a control group) other scholars who took an interest in doing something with Christian and other Abrahamic intellectual traditions, whether they themselves were believers or not. Whatever their religious identities, scholars are scholars, and the way they work reflects the practices of their disciplines. It is in the nature of political theory that political theorists tell other people what to do, even if not all of them are by temperament given to bossing folks around. Historians, in contrast, prefer to describe rather than prescribe. Mark Noll is an intentionally Christian historian, but the history he writes resembles history written by an atheist historian much more closely than philosophy written by a Christian philosopher. But with these disciplinary constants separated out, some interesting patterns emerged among the Erasmus Institute fellows.

First—and perhaps most unsurprising—scholars often favored topics that reflected their own religious commitments or background. One former Erasmus fellow, John McGreevy, an American Catholic from Catholic Notre Dame, has written two books about the history of . . . American Catholics. Another ex-fellow, our editor Thomas Albert Howard, a Protestant from evangelical Gordon College, spent his year at the institute working on Protestant theological faculties in nineteenth-century Germany. Religious affiliation is hardly the only identity that inspires this tendency among scholars. Most historians who write about Italian immigrants in the United States have Italian surnames; a big fraction of scholars of African American literature are themselves African American. Such affinities are of course merely a propensity, far from a universal rule. A (non-Christian) Erasmus fellow from Muslim Turkey worked on medieval Franciscans, while another fellow, *not* of Muslim background, wrote about contemporary Islamic courts. So one unsurprising pattern we see in comparing evangelical and Catholic scholars is a certain gravitation, far from irresistible, toward topics linked to their specific religious faith.

But whatever they write about, evangelicals and Catholics *tend* to differ in line of attack. The verb *tend* requires strong stress. If we tried to graph the methods of individual Catholic and evangelical researchers along a spectrum of religiously inflected approaches to scholarship, the dots would probably scatter all over the place. Nonetheless, the Catholic specks would converge toward a different range of the spectrum from the evangelical points. Max Weber's useful concept of "ideal types" is apt here, and I shall try to describe the ideal types of the evangelical and the Catholic researcher.

Many evangelical scholars approach their research from the specific perspective of Christian faith. A frank acknowledgment of personal faith is far more likely to appear in the preface to a book by an evangelical than in one by a Catholic, and the evangelical is far more likely to try seriously and explicitly to see the subject at hand through the lens of that faith. Often in recent years this faith perspective has reflected the influence of the neo-Calvinism stemming from Abraham Kuyper,[88] even when the scholar in question is not actually Calvinist—an influence mediated through the impressive cadre of historians and philosophers that teach or have once taught at Calvin College. But evangelicals do not need Kuyperian perspectivalism to approach scholar-

88. For helpful introductions to Kuyperian perspectivalism, see Brian J. Walsh and J. Richard Middleton, *The Transforming Vision: Shaping a Christian World View* (Downers Grove, IL: InterVarsity Press, 1984), and Peter S. Heslam, *Creating a Christian World View: Abraham Kuyper's Lectures on Calvinism* (Grand Rapids: Eerdmans, 1998). For an expertly framed taste of Kuyper's own writings, see James D. Bratt, ed., *Abraham Kuyper: A Centennial Reader* (Grand Rapids: Eerdmans, 1998)—the centennial in question being the anniversary of Kuyper's 1898 Stone Lectures at Princeton Theological Seminary.

ship from the point of view of personal faith. Conversations with evangelical colleagues and graduate students suggest that this intellectual habit is so deeply ingrained as to feel second nature to many evangelicals, though it seems far from natural to many Christians from other traditions.

Richard T. Hughes's thoughtful and moving *Vocation of a Christian Scholar* exemplifies the point (even though Hughes's book concerns itself more with teaching than with research). Over a long and influential career, Hughes has labored to develop scholarly and pedagogical practices consonant with and derived from his understanding of the basic tenets of Christian faith. In classes (as he tells us) he always makes sure, without hammering on the point, that students know he is a Christian; he hopes thereby to prod them to think for themselves about the relation of Christianity to their studies. (Inevitably, such hopes are sometimes dashed, as one hilarious episode reminds us.[89] Such is the teacher's lot.) Hughes accepts that his Christian reflections may in the end lead him to practices identical with those of good non-Christian scholar-teachers. The point is not that Christianity should make him behave differently from non-Christian colleagues. The goal is "to allow the presuppositions of the Christian faith to provide the underpinnings and the framework for *how I envision* my work" (my emphasis). Perhaps this approach to Christian scholarship is an academic manifestation of the evangelical stress on the importance of personal witness to faith.[90]

89. When teaching at Abilene Christian University in Texas, Hughes inquired of a class, "If a person asks about the meaning of his or her life, and the answer comes back, 'There is no meaning,' where is that person likely to be in very short order?" Hughes was thinking of the grave; but after a long pause a student finally replied, "The University of Texas?" Hughes, *Vocation of a Christian Scholar*, 81–82.

90. Ibid., 96–98.

For Hughes, it matters more that he conduct his scholarly work within a Christian frame than that his outcomes differ as a result; but many evangelical scholars are certain that their faith does make a substantive difference in their writing. According to the (Christian) historian D. G. Hart, "The conviction that the faith of the Christian historian sets his or her scholarship apart from that produced by the rest of the profession was probably the greatest reason" that evangelicals organized the Conference on Faith and History in 1967. Eventually, Hart argues, as the association grew more professional, its members' clarity diminished about *how* history written by Christians differed from the work of secular historians. But they remained assured that *somehow* a Christian perspective did produce a distinctive kind of history.[91]

The Christian historian and Calvin College émigré George Marsden refines the claim that Christian scholarship is "distinctive." Marsden readily concedes that other scholars might well reach the same conclusions as Christians. But Christian faith does, he contends, equip the scholar with distinctive principles and a distinct perspective. From that standpoint, the Christian scholar will have to reject some theoretical approaches in a given discipline and often may pick out issues that have fallen under the radar of non-Christian scholars. Marsden draws an analogy to feminist scholars, who from feminist principles have developed innovative methodological theories and from a feminist perspective have perceived important subjects previously neglected.[92] The revolution, during my professional lifetime, in the historical understand-

---

91. D. G. Hart, "History in Search of Meaning: The Conference on Faith and History," in *History and the Christian Historian*, ed. Ronald A. Wells (Grand Rapids: Eerdmans, 1998), especially 68 (quotation), 83–84.

92. George M. Marsden, *The Outrageous Idea of Christian Scholarship* (New York: Oxford University Press, 1997).

ing of evangelicalism in nineteenth-century America lends support to Marsden's case. Once treated crudely as an instrument by which elites strove to control the working classes, evangelicalism is now seen by historians as a multifaceted, widely influential cultural phenomenon needing to be grasped in its own terms. In principle, any historian could have spotted the weaknesses in the old interpretation and the superiority of the new one. In fact, it took an "evangelical mafia" (as they used to be called good-naturedly by other American historians)—notable within it Marsden, Noll, and Nathan Hatch—to consider nineteenth-century evangelicalism as more than a capitalist tool. As serious Protestants, these "mafiosi" grasped the import of faith for everyday life and refused to reduce Christianity to an epiphenomenon of social forces or material conditions.

Explicit linkage of faith and research sets such evangelical scholars apart from most nonevangelical colleagues, Christian or no. This evangelical mode of Christian scholarship has the great advantage of keeping research closely in touch with the scholar's deepest commitments and of thus avoiding the intellectual and psychological fragmentation common in modern academic work. The chief drawback is the same: the close tie to Christianity. Explicit linkage of research to Christian faith limits its appeal to—and therefore its influence on—the scholarly world at large. Even the work of so consequential a scholar as George Marsden still sometimes falls under a cloud of suspicion because of his forthright expressions of faith: mistrust usually voiced in conversation rather than reviews, and all the more difficult to counter because underground. That the writings of scholars such as Marsden, Noll, and the neo-Calvinist philosophers Nicholas Wolterstorff and Alvin Plantinga have resonated widely proves that frank statement of one's Christian perspective is not fatal to broader influence. But such open profession does make the hill steeper. The evangelical scholar serious about speaking to her discipline faces a potential dilemma in addressing her audience, a dilemma sometimes heard as "Should I try to publish with [Christian] Eerdmans or [secular] Johns Hopkins University Press?"

Catholic scholars seldom face that particular dilemma— or even whether to publish with Paulist Press or Johns Hopkins. The writings of Catholic scholars (aside from theologians) look, as a rule, like those of scholars with no religious attachments, because Catholics rarely express personal faith in the context of scholarship. Given the traditional Catholic division of labor between laity and clergy, a reader might guess that this reticence originates in Catholic aversion to lay witnessing. Not so: ordained Catholic scholars show the same bent. Walter J. Ong, the great Jesuit student of literature, history, and culture, who died in 2003 at the age of ninety, considered himself a priest first and a teacher-scholar second. He described the Christian scholar's most basic job as witnessing to Christ's presence in the world, by witnessing to it in the scholar's own life and in his relationship to his subject matter. Such witness was how the scholar cooperated in Christ's work of redemption.[93] Ong sometimes wrote on Catholic subjects. But when he wrote on the evolution of consciousness, or on the shift from orality to literacy, or on the sixteenth-century Calvinist logician and pedagogue Petrus Ramus, a reader would not know Ong was Catholic unless she happened to notice the "SJ" after his name on the title page. Why would a dedicated and unembarrassed Catholic priest clam up about his

93. Harry Cargas interview with Walter Ong, April 1975, available at http://rememberingwalterong.com/2003/09/thomas_j_farrell_university_of.html. Ong said that the roles of teacher and scholar were not distinct for him.

religious identity when writing on so value-laden a subject as cultural history?

The answer, I believe, lies principally in the Catholic tradition of universal human reason. That tradition was first fully developed in medieval scholasticism, especially in the writings of Thomas Aquinas. Scholasticism is dead and neo-Thomism a much diminished thing. Yet Catholic intellectuals by and large still share the conviction that in matters of human reason we all stand on the same ground, regardless of religious faith. One might argue that this position resembles the doctrine of common grace as expounded by Kuyperian neo-Calvinists, and it does. But the usual Catholic position is more thoroughgoing. Not merely do Christians and non-Christians share a common realm of human culture and the capacity to work together to improve it. Even more: outside the order of salvation, Christians and non-Christians stand on exactly the same footing: knowledge of reality is accessible to all on the same terms. As far as their scholarship goes, most Catholic intellectuals regard a distinctively "Christian perspective" or "worldview" à la Kuyper—or any other form of perspectivalism—as a weakness to be overcome as much as possible, not as an epistemological inevitability to be embraced with enthusiasm. This is not to say that Catholic universalist views are not grounded in a Christian understanding of reality: they certainly are.

But that Christian understanding of how things are, in its Catholic version, leads to a conviction of the universal power of human reason, equally available to men and women of every culture and faith.[94] Put slightly differently, the "distinc-

94. This traditional Catholic view was rearticulated by John Paul II in the encyclical *Fides et Ratio*, 1998 (http://www.vatican.va/holy_father/john_paul_ii/encyclicals/documents/hf_jp-ii_enc_15101998_fides-et-ratio_en.html. It is entirely characteristic of the tradition that in his introduction the pope invokes ancient Greek and Hindu writings and Chinese sages alongside the Hebrew

Do I think as a Catholic?

tively Christian perspective" of Catholics *is* a universalism that does not single out Christians as intellectually different. Faith gives no *epistemological* edge. When I am writing history—even writing about Christianity—faith does not necessarily make me a better historian or give me any clearer insight into the past. Christianity might make me a *worse* historian, if it biased me against weighing evidence in as clear-eyed a manner as possible. Otherwise, faith bears almost no relevance to my scholarship. "Almost" is a necessary qualification, because Christian faith might inspire the charity toward others that the historian needs in his transactions with the dead, while the Christian conviction of original sin might remind me of my fallibility and the resulting requirement that I keep my mind open to other points of view.[95] But many atheists show more charity and greater humility than a lot of Christians. Such admirable traits may—as belief in original sin might even suggest—owe more to temperament than to conviction.

In any case, this characteristic Catholic contentment with the secular framing of contemporary scholarship probably also reflects the deeply sacramental nature of Catholicism. *Sacramentality* in Catholic thought refers to far more than the seven (as Catholics have it) formal sacraments, from baptism through marriage to the anointing of the sick ("last rites"), though those rituals are certainly central in Catholic sacramental theology. In a broader sense, *sacramentality* denotes the continuing encounter between God and human

---

scriptures. For a recent restatement of this standard outlook in a specifically academic context, see John I. Jenkins, CSC, "A Catholic University in American Academe," in *Remarks from the Academic Conference: The Contribution of Catholic Universities to the Church and Culture, February 1, 2006* (Notre Dame, IN: University of Notre Dame, 2006), 22–24.

95. On this latter point, see the eloquent comments of Richard Hughes in *Vocation of a Christian Scholar*, 29–31.

beings, as always mediated through individual persons and actions. Sometimes that encounter occurs through the ministry of the church. But—though hardly infrequent—ecclesial mediation is the exception, not the rule. Mostly we meet God in everyday life: in our families, in the persons with whom we work, in the work that we do. Or at least so Catholics believe. As Stephen Schloesser writes, "Sacramentality binds us to seeing the finite world as the bearer of the infinite. Or put another way[,] perhaps more importantly: Sacramentality regards the singular with a nearly-infinite significance."[96] In scholarship, this sacramental vision translates into a willingness to take academic institutions and individual scholars on their own, usually secular terms, without any felt urgency about injecting religion explicitly into one's research—any more than, after leaving the library or laboratory, one would approach umpiring a Little League game "from a Christian perspective." The evangelical scholar Richard Hughes concisely summarizes the point when he explains that a sacramental view "allows Catholic educators to take the world seriously on its own terms and to interact with the world as it is." Hughes goes on to quote Alice Gallin, OSU, longtime head of the Association of Catholic Colleges and Universities, to the effect that " 'secular' is not simply nor always the opposite of 'sacred,' for in a Christian sacramental view of reality, the secular has a legitimate role and one that is congruent with and not opposed to faith or religion."[97]

Faith, then, seems largely irrelevant for the normal tasks of the typical Catholic scholar (again excepting the theolo-

---

96. Manuscript, 1997, quoted in Clarke E. Cochran, "Institutions and Sacraments: The Catholic Tradition and Political Science," in *Religion, Scholarship, and Higher Education*, ed. Sterk, 135. Cochran and Schloesser were both Erasmus Fellows in 1998–99.

97. Hughes, *Vocation of a Christian Scholar*, 45 (quoting a manuscript by Gallin).

gian); but "religious affiliation" or "religious traditions" or "religious knowledge" may be very much to the point. A Christian historian might write more perceptively about the history of Christianity than an atheist or a Buddhist because she knows more about Christianity. And any historian might also learn things from her Christian background helpful in analyzing historical problems more acutely, even when those problems have nothing to do with Christianity. When Catholic scholars take explicit advantage of their religious commitments, it is usually in this second-hand way. But "religious commitments" is not *le mot juste*: a phrase like "religious background" is more apt. For such scholars do not appeal to personal faith but rather learn from intellectual or aesthetic or social or ritual traditions of Catholicism. A lapsed Catholic well versed in his former religion would, in this view, be better placed as a scholar than a poorly informed practicing Catholic.

Research drawing in this way on Catholic traditions has no transcendent reference, but neither is it trivial for the earthly work of learning. An example may make the point.[98] The Roman Church never warmed up to the idea of sovereign nation-states, in part because national states threatened the church's own universalist claims, in part because sovereign assertion of absolute government power imperiled the autonomy of individual souls in their relation to their Creator. So Catholic thinkers developed, from the sixteenth century onward, in parallel with the tradition of sovereignty in secular political theory, a counter-tradition that rejected the idea of pure sovereignty in favor of multitiered ways of conceptualizing government power. The principle of subsidiarity,

98. This and part of the next paragraph adapt and rearrange language from James Turner, "Does Religion Have Anything Worth Saying to Scholars?" in *Religion, Scholarship, and Higher Education*, ed. Sterk, 18–19.

first clearly articulated in Catholic teaching 115 years ago,[99] states that public duties should be spread across a spectrum of public authorities—ranging from individuals and families through private groups and institutions, local administrations, and national governments, up to international agencies. The lowest competent authority should always have priority in acting and always in service to the human person rather than to the state. This principle of subsidiarity played a pivotal role in the constitutional arrangements of the European Union.[100] The principle of subsidiarity, and the broader intellectual tradition from which it came, are now proving helpful to political scientists as they cope with analyzing the world today: a world in which regional devolution, on the one hand, and supragovernmental entities like the UN and NGOs and multinational corporations, on the other, make hash of the traditional idea of sovereignty as the regnant category for understanding "the state."[101]

But Catholic traditions interact with contemporary scholarship in less explicitly theoretical ways. Caroline Bynum, in her eulogy for the distinguished medieval historian David Herlihy (a Catholic), spoke of Herlihy's role as pioneer of women's history in medieval studies. She traced his innovations back to Herlihy's interest in the discourse of spiritual friendship of men and women in the monastic tradition.[102]

99. By Leo XIII in the encyclical *Rerum Novarum* (1891), developed further by Pius XI in his encyclical *Quadragesimo Anno* (1931) and more recently by John Paul II in *Centisimus Annus* (1991).

100. First in the Treaty of Maastricht, 1993. Cf. the discussion at http://www.euractiv.com/en/constitution/future-eu-subsidiarity/article-117271. For a skeptical view of the European Union's application of the principle, see Antonio Estella, *The EU Principle of Subsidiarity and Its Critique* (Oxford: Oxford University Press, 2002).

101. E.g., Heinz-Gerhard Justenhoven and James Turner, eds., *Rethinking the State in the Age of Globalisation: Catholic Thought and Contemporary Political Theory*, Politik: Forschung und Wissenschaft 10 (Münster: LIT-Verlag, 2003).

102. Personal information.

To offer another case: Catholicism is, as already mentioned, a strongly sacramental religion, and Catholics are apt to see intimations of the divine in ceremonies as simple as lighting candles and in physical material as odd as the holy dirt (supposed to heal the sick and the lame) in the sacristy of the chapel of Chimayo in northern New Mexico. "The sacramental vision," as Clarke Cochran has written, "posits that God is encountered in material things, in signs imbued with the living presence of the hidden God. . . . In this tradition, sacramentality is not limited to the seven sacraments, but is the life of the church itself. . . . The Catholic encounter with God takes place not simply in the depth of conscience, but is mediated by historical, material institutions."[103] In thinking in this way, Catholics are not unlike Jews, for whom encounter with the divine is similarly mediated by eating bitter herbs or by blowing a shofar (ram's horn). Protestants, in contrast, have tended to see papist superstition in this sort of stuff. Maybe this is why few Protestants found a place among the twentieth-century anthropologists who taught us about the social efficacy of symbolism. Victor Turner's Catholicism clearly inflected his studies of ritual.[104] Mary Douglas, perhaps the greatest symbolic anthropologist of the later twentieth century, reminisced in old age about the continuous internal dialogue between her Catholicism and her anthropological writings.[105] Yet if you read her greatest work, *Purity and*

103. Clarke E. Cochran, "Sacrament and Solidarity: Catholic Social Thought and Health Care Policy Reform," *Journal of Church and State* 41 (1999): 492.

104. Mathieu Deflem, "Ritual, Anti-Structure, and Religion: A Discussion of Victor Turner's Processual Symbolic Analysis," *Journal for the Scientific Study of Religion* 30 (1991): 1–25, available at http://www.cas.sc.edu/socy/faculty/deflem/zturn.htm.

105. See Mary Douglas, "A Feeling for Hierarchy," in *Believing Scholars: Ten Catholic Intellectuals*, ed. James L. Heft, SM (New York: Fordham University Press, 2005).

Danger (1966), you will find no explicit reference to her faith. That silence is typical of Catholics.

As with characteristic evangelical approaches to scholarship, there is a downside and an upside to these Catholic habits. An intellectual dialogue between religious tradition and research agenda has little to do with vital faith. Catholic scholars may risk losing hold of the living link between their scholarship and their personal faith, putting faith in one box and their intellectual life in another. But when Catholic scholars make use of Catholic traditions, they tend to use them in ways accessible to, even appealing to, nonreligious readers. So this style of work gives Catholic ways of thinking and behaving some purchase on larger intellectual life. This stimulus can even create in the penumbra beyond Christianity a certain openness or receptivity to Christianity and Christian values.[106] Apparently Victor Turner's realization that functionalist interpretations of ritual did not begin to address its most important meanings helped to lead him away from Marxism and into Catholic Christianity.[107]

In contrasting these Catholic with evangelical approaches to teaching and to research, I have, to repeat, been examining tendencies and leanings. There is nothing exclusive about either evangelical or Catholic characteristics. Some evangelical scholars behave "like Catholics" in the terms laid out above, while some Catholic academics (fewer, I think) act "like evangelicals." Nor is there any burglar alarm to prevent one group from raiding the other's refrigerator.

Indeed, in learned practice today, once-customary ecclesial boundaries can grow very blurred. How blurred is demonstrated in a penetrating recent book by the evangelical

---

106. This fits roughly with what Catholics mean by "evangelizing the culture." Cf. Jenkins, "Catholic University in American Academe," 24.

107. Deflem, "Ritual, Anti-Structure, and Religion."

literary scholar Roger Lundin of Wheaton College, entitled
From Nature to Experience: The American Search for Cultural Authority.[108] Perhaps the book also exemplifies how
evangelicals and Catholics can learn from each other, since
Lundin wrote the first draft as a senior fellow of the Erasmus Institute, in a year when members of those two groups
dominated the fellowships—though Lundin would have to
speak for himself about any such cross-fertilization. For
present purposes, we can put to one side his argument: an
acute assessment of the ironies and dilemmas of American
pragmatism, broadly construed.

What matters now is his broader argumentative strategy. Lundin makes clear that he writes as a Christian—as
evangelical scholars in the human sciences often do make
clear. And he uses Christian theology (most notably Karl
Barth's) as an analytic tool to help him work through the
cultural tribulations that are his theme. But Lundin says, in
effect: Look, reader, you need not be a Christian to follow
my analysis. When using, say, Foucault's ideas, we rarely inquire into the validity of his underlying metaphysical axioms;
we just see whether he can help us figure a way out of the
intellectual problem at hand. So, too, forget about whether
you, reader, believe in the God whom Barth writes about.
Let us simply find out if the Christian point of view can help
us to see more clearly our way through the implications of
"experience" as a source of cultural authority.

It strikes me that Lundin has wedded some typically evangelical and characteristically Catholic modes of bringing
Christianity to bear on scholarship. He bears witness to his
own faith, and he draws on Christian intellectual traditions.
But he invites readers to consider these traditions apart from

108. *From Nature to Experience: The American Search for Cultural Authority*
(Lanham, MD: Rowman and Littlefield, 2005).

faith. Still, some unbelieving readers who carefully follow Lundin to the end of his story will come away with second thoughts about their dismissal of Christianity as a scholarly resource—and with deepened respect for the Christian scholar, on however remote a planet he may seem to dwell. That is not so unpromising an ending.

III

The Responses

Response to "Reconsidering Christendom?"

By James Turner

A few admirable scholars wear immense learning lightly. Mark Noll is one of them. And make no mistake, profound historical and theological erudition lie behind his thoughtful contribution to our dialogue. Yet it strikes me that my own account skates on the surface of the same deep waters he plumbs. Where I try to sketch a few main lines of the relationship today of evangelical and Catholic higher learning, Noll offers a sweeping, centuries-long overview that explains how the present situation arose. For the most part, we agree on what the main issues are, what is at stake, and what the future will likely hold. But Noll raises a couple of questions on which we may differ. These issues merit brief exploration, precisely because we see eye to eye about so much else.

The first of these questions concerns the parallelism between evangelicalism and Catholicism. Noll and I both presume that these two entities can be fruitfully compared. The very title of our original dialogue, *Evangelicalism, Catholicism, and the Future of Christian Learning* presupposes such comparison. There is one odd feature, then, of Noll's otherwise compelling story of the evolution of Christian learning from the Reformation to the present day. During most of the narrative, Catholicism is present, evangelicalism (in our sense) absent. Noll must measure Catholicism, rather, against Protestantism at large and, specifically, against magisterial Protestantism embodied in established churches (as distinct from Anabaptist traditions). Only when reaching the last century does he (can he) start to compare Catholicism with evangelicalism. The institutional analogy between the magisterial established churches and the Roman Catholic church is reasonably clear. But American evangelicalism is a horse of a very different color from magisterial Protestantism. So the shift is a little jarring. It makes us think.

For one thing, it makes us think about what holds Catholicism together and what holds evangelicalism together, each perhaps just tightly enough that we can call it by a single name. The glues are of radically dissimilar composition. "Catholicism" exists because a single institutional church houses all Catholics and provides for them a common sacramental worship. Otherwise, contemporary Roman Catholics fall all over the place in terms of their theology, their ecclesiology, their understanding of the Bible, their degree of institutional loyalty, their moral tenets, and so forth. The Vatican can publish a catechism, but no pope can make Catholics read it, much less assent to everything it says. Catholics may be required to believe defined dogmas, such as papal infallibility, but many exempt themselves from the requirement. American bishops wave before their flocks mandatory prohibitions of assorted sexual delinquencies, and the sheep frolic as if the bishops had ordered contraception and premarital cohabitation. Rome's ever more strenuous insistence on an all-male priesthood only seems to embolden advocates of women's ordination.

Evangelicals have no pope and no Vatican, yet in real-world terms they have a stronger theological center of gravity than Catholics do: that center, indeed, defines them. It would be ludicrous to minimize what divides evangelicals. The fruitfulness of evangelicals in inventing new denominations and subdividing old ones is a perpetual wonder to undergraduates taking courses on American religious history. (If I may indulge in personal nostalgia, my mother's people were Missionary Baptists from Kentucky, a state whose Baptist sects alone once may have outnumbered all the varieties of Christianity across Europe. It is a sad thing that much of this purebred American idiosyncrasy has withered in the age of the megachurch—but by no means all of it.) And no one attending a Pentecostal service could possibly mistake it for worship at the local Church of Christ. Nor does one readily imagine Ron Sider and Richard Land running on the same ticket. And yet. Why do we call all of these folks "evangelicals," and why do they so label themselves? It is solely because they share certain core beliefs—about the Bible, about new birth in Christ, about the awakened Christian's duty to spread the good news. Catholics do not agree among themselves about a single one of those items. But, then, they do not need to in order to be "Catholics." The very structure of being "evangelical" and being "Catholic" could hardly differ more sharply.

Despite this difference, it remains possible and helpful to compare these apples and oranges in the orchards of higher learning. Catholic and evangelical academics do in fact cooperate, and in the world of scholarship they puzzle over many of the same dilemmas. This bare fact proves that the two groups have enough in common to make it worth inquiring into what they share and where that sharing stops. But Noll's acute analysis also has the ironic effect of persuading me that neither one of us has analyzed acutely enough. Surely this difference in the fundamental character of these two Christian traditions must ramify through their adherents' academic work in ways that call for further inquiry. I suspect, though I cannot specify, that there is more to be said—more, in particular, than I have said—about the differential grounding of Catholic and evangelical higher learning in the differential natures of what holds each of these religious traditions together.

Evangelicals and Catholics do come together, of course, in one essential matter. They share, with other Christians, the fundamentals of doctrine hammered out in the ecumenical councils of the early church and proclaimed in the Nicene Creed. These basic beliefs provide, in the actual context of American colleges and universities, a broad swath of common ground.

Mark Noll argues that Christian learning must be genuinely Christian in this sense, founded on a trinitarian understanding of God. Such a criterion makes a lot of sense, but let us see where it leads us. Consider Andrews Norton. Norton (1786–1853) is not a household name today, except in my household, so a few biographical words are in order. He was one of the earliest serious biblical scholars in the United States. He drew from the wells of German learning, but he defended the Bible as the Word of God against leading German biblical critics of his day, whose writings (at least in Norton's view) undermined the Bible's authority. His magnum opus was a three-volume *Genuineness of the Gospels* (1837–44). Its title sums up its message, and it won praise on both sides of the English-speaking Atlantic. Seen in the perspective of the ages, Andrews Norton was not really a great scholar, but he was a pretty good one for his time and place. A devout man, his piety shining through the many hymns he wrote, Norton believed himself undeniably a Christian scholar. And who would quarrel with him about that? Mark Noll would, for Andrews Norton was a Unitarian.

Do we exclude him—and others like him—by definition? If so, then what about his three fat volumes? If Norton was not a Christian scholar, does *The Genuineness of the Gospels*—admired by orthodox Presbyterian and Congregationalist intellectuals in its day—count nevertheless as Christian scholarship? Or take a more extreme comparison. My Notre Dame colleague George Marsden, a well-known Christian scholar by any standard, recently published a superb biography of Jonathan Edwards, at once immensely well informed, deeply sympathetic, and critically distanced. No one would doubt that Marsden's *Edwards* counts as first-rate Christian learning. More than half a century ago, the late Perry Miller published his great trilogy on Edwards's theological predecessors, the New England Puritans. It was also immensely well informed, deeply sympathetic, and critically distanced. While revised in many details by subsequent historians (as perhaps Marsden's book will have been fifty years from now), Miller's work remains the fundamental starting point for understanding these American Calvinists. Unlike Marsden, Perry Miller was not a Calvinist. He was, in fact, an atheist who did not believe a word of those Puritan doctrines about which he wrote with such enormous insight and appreciation. Do we call his work "Christian learning"?

To frame the issue squarely, you can imagine two works of historical (or literary or sociological or anthropological) scholarship sitting side by side on your bookshelf. Both concern Christian themes. Both employ perspectives derived from Christianity. Both approach Christianity with the critical empathy required to conduct research in the human sciences. But you have not had time to check on the authors' church membership. You are helpless—by Noll's definition—to determine whether either of these books qualifies as Christian learning. Then at last you discover that the author of the first is a faithful Baptist while the author of the second is an agnostic who lolls around on Sunday morning sipping coffee and reading the *New York Times*. Magically the first book becomes Christian scholarship, and the second drops out of the running. But—oops—you got it backwards. It turns out actually to be the first author who is curled up with the *Times* when she should be in church, and the *second* author who is the devout Baptist. *Now* the second book is Christian learning, and the first secular scholarship.

This exercise may seem too much like a shell game to be fair to Noll, but there is a serious issue at stake: is Christian *learning* a subset of Christian *faith*, or can nonbelievers contribute to Christian learning? I do not mean, can Christians in the academy learn from non-Christians? The answer to that question is so obvious as to be trivial. I mean, rather, can scholars who do not accept Christianity, or even believe in God, engage in Christian scholarship as full participants? The answer to *that* question may, at first, seem equally obvious. To assert that a non-Christian can produce Christian scholarship appears admittedly oxymoronic. But change the terms. Can a non-Russian compose Russian scholarship? Can a historian in the twenty-first century write fifteenth-century history? The matter no longer seems quite so clear-cut. Does the adjective *Christian* in the phrase *Christian learning* refer to the scholar or the scholarship?

We can pursue this conundrum further along somewhat different lines. Noll observes that "when foundational commitments in ethics, epistemology, and metaphysics play a role in shaping and interpreting research, the Christian factor in Christian learning becomes more salient." That claim is not merely plausible but seems at first intuitively right. And if you happen to be a Kuyperian neo-Calvinist, then maybe you do have certain epistemological commitments that set you apart from non-Christians—indeed, from most non-Kuyperians. But even if we limit "Christian scholars" to those who fit Noll's criterion of believers in the three-personed God, not all of them are Kuyperian neo-Calvinists. And among those who are not Kuyperians, the Christian foundational commitments in ethics, epistemology, and metaphysics that shape their research in perceptible ways rarely seem exclusively Christian. (I leave aside the special cases of research in theology and in philosophy of religion.) Let us think for a moment about the doctrine of creation. It is the Christian metaphysical commitment with possibly the most wide-ranging implications for learning (and for Christian epistemological tenets). But Jews and Muslims share the Christian understanding of creation, and the Jews got there first. A Christian conception of human nature prevents Christian scholars from taking rational-choice theory as a full account of human behavior (whatever its analytic uses). But such a conception of human nature is hardly unique to Christians. Maybe some uniquely Christian foundational commitment—say, trinitarianism—could mold historical or literary learning. But I am hard pressed to say how, and I have yet to see a work of nontheological, nonphilosophical scholarship in which I could detect the footprints of trinitarianism.

If my arguments hold water, we have not discovered, up to this point in our reflections, any way in which Christian faith is prerequisite to Christian learning—no matter how large a role faith plays in the life of the Christian individual who pursues the learning. Tangible products of scholarship by believing Christians cannot reliably be distinguished from similar works by nonbelievers. Ontological, epistemological, and moral commitments that perceptibly shape the scholarship of believing Christians are widely shared by non-Christians. Is there, then, no way in which Christianity distinctively molds learning (outside of theology and philosophy of religion)?

Of course there is a way, and I detailed some of its markers in my essay for this volume. As every historian must insist, we are all shaped by history, including notably our personal histories. For Christians, these personal histories teem with religious experiences (among other kinds). When Mark Noll or I sit down to write as professional historians, we each bring to our task perspectives and mental habits forged in the circumstances of our own lives. This personal baggage includes our past as Christians. (This past, I strongly suspect, has heavier weight in shaping our scholarship than does our self-conscious present.) Packed into the luggage we carry is everything from the ways we learned to worship to the language of the hymns we sang. Now, these sorts of influences are not generically "Christian." Christianity does not come in generic form—pace C. S. Lewis's "mere Christianity." If a Christian's religious formation significantly inflects the labor of learning, the product of his work will thus be "Catholic scholarship" or "Presbyterian erudition" or "evangelical learning," not some nonspecific Christian scholarship. Nonetheless, here we do see a genuine and distinctive Christian influence on scholarship: the quarry we have been hunting for the last few pages. I suggested earlier that a peculiarly Catholic sacramental understanding of the world haunts the writings of some Catholic scholars. I strongly suspect that my own high school formation by Jesuits left an ineradicable mark on my approach to writing history, though to fill out this speculation would need more space than available here and, anyway, might interest only one or two elderly priests.

But let us presume that the effects of a Catholic formation shine forth from every page I write; still, this afterglow will not light our way back to Noll's insistence that Christian learning must be genuinely Christian. A Catholic formation—or an evangelical one—notoriously comes with no warranty. University faculties are, like the world at large, littered with fallen-away Catholics, ex-evangelicals, former Methodists, one-time Episcopalians, and middle-aged Baptists who found Christ as fourteen-year-olds and last went to church as college freshmen. The academic study of religion seems to attract these "exes" in especially large proportion. And probably their Christian formation helps to make them good at it: they know about religion. Likewise, not only the knowledge but also the attitudes, the sensitivities, the ethic one develops through a thorough formation in any faith will generally endure even if the faith withers.

These things become part of who one is, and they cannot help but influence how one approaches scholarship. Mary Douglas, as it happened, persisted as a believing Catholic Christian. But her convent-school education and her sacramentally formed sensitivity to symbolic meanings would have stayed with her even if she had lost her faith soon after she matriculated in Oxford. To sum up all of my doubts about Mark Noll's really admirable insistence that Christian learning must be genuinely Christian: I can see only one way in which Christianity can exert a distinctive, shaping influence on learning, and this way requires only that the scholar once have been Christian, not that she still live in faith. The identifiably "Christian" scholar—identifiable, that is, by her scholarly works—must have somehow been molded by Christianity but need no longer believe in it.

Possibly, Catholics may find themselves more comfortable with this conclusion than evangelicals—for reasons related to the query I raised at the beginning of these comments on Noll's argument. If Catholics construct their religious identity more in terms of affiliation with an institution and its tradition, and if evangelicals think of theirs more in terms of voluntary personal beliefs, then the "faith content" of "Christian learning" may loom larger to evangelicals, may even seem essential. Catholics may fret less about the current beliefs of a given scholar, since they can perhaps more readily imagine themselves losing their faith but retaining a significant degree of Catholic identity.

This issue of the connection of Christian faith to Christian learning, in any case, is not a trivial matter of semantics. It determines whom we accept as fellow workers in the vineyard of Christian learning. Or, to shift the metaphor, it is not a matter of how strictly we can police borders. It is a matter of whether discernible boundaries exist. If a vast, gray frontier of disputed territory divides two nations, neither can usefully employ a border patrol.

Response to "Enduring Differences, Blurring Boundaries"

By Mark A. Noll

The depth of James Turner's programmatic wisdom is evident in every section of his contribution. Of course, since I have been trained in the academic culture that Turner, quite rightly, records as having exerted such a strong influence on all American academics of a certain age (namely, his and mine), I am prepared to pick as many nits as space would allow. For example, Turner writes that "a reader would not know [Walter J.] Ong was a Catholic" simply from reading his books on orality and literacy, the logician Petrus Ramus, or the evolution of consciousness—except perhaps if one noticed the 'SJ' tacked on to his name on the title page." This statement may be technically correct, but my experience with some of these books left me convinced that I could *guess* that Ong's treatments reflected the work not only of a "baptized imagination" but of a specifically Catholic intelligence.

On a broader plane, Turner concedes that "the Christian conviction of original sin" might make at least a slight difference in the scholarship of Roman Catholics who hold that conviction. From my angle, original sin could never play such a trivial role. If it is true that, in Milton's phrase, "man's first disobedience . . . brought death into the world, and all our woe," then everything must in some way be touched by that reality. For academic purposes, it is probably not necessary to make original sin the determinative crux for everything—physics as much as art history, mathematics as well as psychology—as some determined Augustinians have done. Yet a central truth of the great Augustinian tradition is to recognize that the human delight in divine grace (with all the hope it entails) is always coordinate with the human perception of human need (with all the self-deception it entails). So for academics who study the human condition or human actions, or for those who study the human student studying such things, original sin can never be only an incidental matter. Moreover, if original sin is a central rather than just an incidental fact, then the divine gifts that have overcome it—which is to say the redeeming work of God in the intention of the Father, the action of the Son, and the presence of the Holy Spirit—must, by their nature, be as relevant to scholarship as to all other human enterprises.

So it could go for quite a while. Yet to pursue the nitpicking path would be to neglect Turner's stellar assessment of recent and current efforts by both evangelicals and Catholics—or at least *some* evangelicals and *some* Catholics—to function as Christian scholars, to cooperate with each other in some enterprises, and, while cooperating with each other, also to cooperate with those who do not share their Christian traditions. On these matters Turner's account of the current state of play is more perceptive than anything I have ever seen.

The array of his insights is stunning. Turner has said no more than the truth when he notes the strong influence of contemporary American culture on all aspects of learning, including all forms of Christian learning. He is especially perceptive about the particular kind of cultural influence that has been exerted in the academy by the standards of professionalization that came to dominate the American middle classes after World War II. As Turner points out, once professional standards have been internalized—as they have, to at least considerable degree, within all institutions of Christian higher education, from the most self-effacing bivocational seminaries and Bible schools to the best-funded and most prestigious universities—then all considerations of "Christian learning" must also involve consideration of the cultures in which it occurs.

An insight that bears on the future grows from Turner's experience as director of Notre Dame's Erasmus Institute. The fact that the institute found it easier to enlist scholars from history, literature, philosophy, and political thought than from all other disciplines cries out for investigation. Why were these fields overrepresented? Is it something related to the contemporary practices of these disciplines? something intrinsic to Christian faith? something growing from the networks of scholars who happen to be active in these fields? Finding answers to such questions would seem to offer at least a few clues to those who plot the way ahead, for it would allow a measure of informed planning oriented to realities about the task at hand.

On the possibility of institutional cooperation between Catholics and evangelicals, Turner has concluded forthrightly, but with as much gentleness as possible, that extensive mutual activity is not likely, given the relative place of the schools in the public pecking orders that receive so much attention—which, of course, no one takes seriously, except for purposes of student recruitment, budget priorities, presidential selection, faculty assessment, and institutional self-confidence! He has also pointed out that in the spectrum of possible approaches to Christian higher education, Catholic institutions are gathered strongly toward the "open" end and evangelical institutions cluster toward the "particular" end, which yields a situation making extensive institutional alignment all but impossible.

This observation leads Turner to especially shrewd comments on commonalities and differences in approaches to learning. If Christian learning for Catholics is rooted in a religious tradition defined by liturgy, hierarchy, and sacraments, then significant strain is inevitable when cooperation looms with evangelicals who are rooted in a religion of personal decision for Christ and personal relationship with Christ.

Turner rightly notes that American evangelicals have received a major assist in their academic efforts by the neo-Calvinism broadening from Abraham Kuyper through Calvin College to many points on the evangelical landscape. That insight could be carried further to underscore his sense of significant difference between Catholic and evangelical traditions. As it happens, Kuyper's notion of "sphere sovereignty" bears certain similarities to the principle of subsidiarity developed by Pope Leo XIII and subsequent Catholic thinkers. As versions of "sphere sovereignty" have worked their way through the evangelical academy, they have helped some evangelicals in moving on to study Catholic concepts of natural law and also subsidiarity itself. The interesting historical point, which Turner does record, is that American evangelicals have been assisted in their consideration of such matters by the strand in evangelicalism that is least conversionistic,

most self-consciously traditional, most seriously catecheti-
cal, and most ecclesiastical. In other words, one of the most
academically productive bridges between Catholics and
evangelicals has been built by one of the least typical forms
of evangelicalism.

Turner's general analysis hinges on the critically important
observation that he states explicitly in at least two places:
"Catholic and evangelical faith traditions are very different
in character" and "evangelicals and Catholics *tend* to differ
in line of attack."

In my view, these succinct observations are entirely correct, and they define both the difficulties and the potential
for the current moment in Catholic-evangelical academic
relations. They deserve a great deal of reflection.

The reality for Catholic and evangelical academics, as
for Catholic and evangelical traditions as a whole, is that
Catholicism and evangelicalism represent two quite different forms of Christianity. In another place I have tried
to describe these different forms as analogous to distinct
language groups.[109] The intriguing thing about the present is
that where once everyone was sure that these languages were
as distinct as Hungarian and French, now more and more
have come around to the opinion that they may more closely
resemble Dutch and Norwegian. The situation that prevailed
from the mid-sixteenth century, when historians like the
Lutheran John Sleidan or the Huguenot Lancelot du Voisin,
sieur de la Popelinière, were excoriated by both Catholics
and Protestants for their sin of writing with charity about
both strands,[110] to the very recent past is largely gone. After

109. Mark A. Noll and Carolyn Nystrom, *Is the Reformation Over? An Evangelical Assessment of Contemporary Evangelicalism* (Grand Rapids: Baker Academic, 2005), 240–47.

110. A. G. Dickens and John M. Tonkin, *The Reformation in Historical Thought*
(Cambridge, MA: Harvard University Press, 1985), 16, 84.

the Second Vatican Council, after the evangelical rebound from the separatistic excesses of fundamentalism, after the ad hoc alliances thrown up by recent political battles, after the pan-Christian edification absorbed from figures like Karl Barth, Hans Urs von Balthasar, John Meyendorff, and a host of ancient church fathers, after so many positive Catholic-Protestant encounters in so many local neighborhoods—after all these experiences, it is impossible not to realize that a new day has dawned. Even the academically inclined should be able to see it.

So we have evangelical literary critics like Roger Lundin in whose scholarship Turner can discern some characteristics hitherto more common among Roman Catholics and yet integrated with Lundin's own evangelical convictions. For myself, I can read entire paragraphs, sometimes whole pages, from John Paul II and Benedict XVI and be convinced that they could have come from a book published by Inter-Varsity Press.

What Turner has done so well in his chapter is focus the questions being posed for teaching, research, and institutional practice from this new situation: the partial convergence of long-standing Christian traditions that are no longer as antithetical as they once seemed to be, the remaining circumstances that continue to differentiate the two unmistakably, the forms of cooperation that are now possible and that remain impossible, and the multiplying instances of manifest, if also ambiguous, commonality.

The situation that Turner has described so well is big with implications—for younger scholars choosing research strategies and discovering their own natural faith communities, for older scholars both drawn to and skittish about new possibilities across the Catholic-evangelical border, for the many believing scholar-teachers in American colleges and universities who feel isolated from all Christian connections, and, not least, for deans, provosts, presidents, and trustees of Christian institutions. If the latter do what they should do, they must balance faithfulness to their institutions' particular traditions with aggressive exploitation of the deeper Christian possibilities opened up by Catholic-evangelical engagement.

What, given this situation, should be done to advance Christian learning? Historians are not adept at predicting the future, but we do record things that really take place. So here are three journalistic snapshots—call them instant histories—that may show whence things have come and where things may go.

First story: Not too many years ago I was privileged to attend a small gathering where everyone else present was either a practicing Catholic or a birth Catholic who, if not practicing, retained some identification with the church. The task was to reflect on connections between the faith in which the participants had been raised, and most still practiced, and their work as historians. My role, I think, was to serve as a sympathetic, if often clueless, Protestant kibbutzer and, more specifically, to defend the views that George Marsden had published about the nature of Christian scholarship when those views were subjected to criticism, as happened with some frequency. At a couple of points along the way, I tentatively raised questions about how a historian's personal beliefs or personal piety ought to affect that historian's teaching and scholarship. Only one of the Catholics responded to these queries, and did so with unusual insight. But for the most part, my questions received from the group only a series of indulgent blank looks. As the meeting went on, I found out that the one other participant who was interested in questions that concerned me had grown up in a

Presbyterian church of decidedly evangelical leanings before becoming a Catholic as a young adult.

Second story: Also a few years ago, I was asked to give a short presentation on my approach to scholarship at one of a series of meetings sponsored by a generous philanthropy on the subject of religion and higher education. It is important to stress that by the time this particular meeting rolled around, the regular participants had grown quite friendly, though it was a diverse group made up of Catholics of several stripes, Lutherans, Baptists, undifferentiated evangelicals, several Jews, and a few professed unbelievers. My presentation advanced the thesis that, at least in some carefully qualified sense, all real learning must by its nature reflect not just the general truths of Christianity but in some specific way the presence of Jesus Christ (see John 1:3 or Col. 1:16–17). To this proposal at least one of the Jewish scholars responded that he could see, given my Christian starting point, how I might make such a claim. But then one of the senior Catholic participants chimed in with a forceful, articulate, and unequivocal objection. "Nonsense," if I recall correctly, was one of the gentler judgments.

Beyond being a trifle ruffled by the vigor of this second response, I was also bemused, precisely because of why I held this Catholic scholar in such high regard. I had found his writing to be persuasive, but I also cherished the memory of a striking moment from yet another conference a few years before. In this earlier meeting, which was organized by several high-powered secular intellectuals, my Catholic friend was making a presentation about the aspirations of leading figures of the Enlightenment. In preparing to deliver his own opinions about the writings of one of them, this scholar began a sentence with an arresting dependent clause: "If you believe in original sin," he said; then

he paused, defiantly raised his head, and said slowly and
distinctly, "which I do," and then went on to the sentence's
main clause and the rest of his talk. But then, a few years
later, when I thought I was doing something like the same
thing, I found out differently.

Third story: My late friend and colleague George Rawlyk
was a Canadian historian who, as a Baptist socialist, inhab-
ited a sphere that I had thought, based on my American
experience, was a null set. Rawlyk's intellectual and personal
journey was sui generis. Although the Ukrainian immigrant
household in which he was raised was not churchgoing,
it was strongly influenced by Orthodox traditions. It was
also strongly influenced by socialist-labor convictions. As
a teenager, Rawlyk was converted to an evangelical form of
Christianity through the work of an unmarried female missionary who operated a kind of Baptist settlement house in
his lower-class neighborhood. When he became a professional historian of the early Maritime Provinces, Rawlyk's
mentors taught him to analyze events in primarily economi-
cal and political terms, despite the fact that Maritime history
in his period included several evangelical revivals of broad
influence. For the first half of his professional life, which led
him eventually to the chair in history at Queen's University, Rawlyk carried out his research keyed to economic and
political interpretations—while he functioned personally as
an active Baptist layman, an active supporter of the socialist
New Democratic Party, and an active sponsor of evangelical
student groups like InterVarsity Christian Fellowship.

Only at midcareer did Rawlyk discover how to bring the
parts of his life together. Yet not until reading James Turner's
essay did I realize the significance of what happened in the
integration of Rawlyk's personal and professional interests.
That integration took place when two intellectual influences

reshaped his treatment of eighteenth-century Maritime history. The first was George Marsden, especially Marsden's *Fundamentalism and American Culture*, from which Rawlyk discerned how a practicing evangelical might write sympathetically, and yet with historical integrity, about episodes in the past when something like the author's own evangelical faith was prominent. The second influence was conveyed by the anthropological studies of Victor Turner, especially his treatment of religious rituals. By enlisting Marsden and Turner together, Rawlyk's career as a historian turned a corner. His written work, while continuing to benefit from earlier economic and political emphases, began to show how the rituals of evangelical revival could be presented as solid history to both believing and secular readers. After thinking about James Turner's essay, it strikes me that Rawlyk's development as a historian can be explained only as a result of cooperation between evangelical and Catholic learning—in cooperation with insights from those who were not believers of any sort.

What do I take from these three stories? First, differences between Catholic and evangelical Christians are real differences that affect academic matters as surely as everything else. If Catholics and evangelicals are no longer isolated from each other, it is nonetheless intellectually obdurate to regard them as simply two variations of a common Christianity.

Second, since characteristic differences between Catholic and evangelical academics are rooted—as James Turner has shown so well—in core beliefs and practices, then those differences are not going to vanish speedily.

Yet, third, the recent situation of fruitful exchange between Catholics and evangelicals opens nearly unprecedented opportunities for fruitful interaction. If Walter Ong's brilliant treatment of Ramist logic is somehow connected to his Catholic identity—but at deep levels of a type hard for evangelicals to figure out—then making the effort to figure out what Ong did may possibly help one or two evangelical scholars learn something about previously unexamined possibilities for Christian learning—and maybe even about previously unexamined possibilities for the Christian faith itself. If George Marsden's willingness, as a layperson, to theologize about the nature of modern scholarship encourages a few Catholic historians to do the same thing (or to do it better), his example will have led the way toward some of the same possibilities.

Fourth, what I take away most from the stories I have related, even more from James Turner's splendid contribution, but most of all from the fact that there are now so many mutual explorations of the sort represented by this book—is the marvel, which has come to pass in the short span of my academic life, of Catholics and evangelicals' actually talking to and with each other about issues of mutual intellectual concern. If the talk is still halting, if communication is still blurred, if insubstantial enthusiasms or fearful apprehensions are still all too common, nonetheless the convergence is taking place, and right before our eyes. As the case of George Rawlyk demonstrates, the consequences can make a real difference.

Where are things headed? No historian can say. But what the current situation opens up are startling possibilities for scholar-teachers, for administrators who guide institutions, for students, and for all who value the life of the mind. Turner's essay is as good a marking of the journey to this point as one can imagine. As a Catholic he would perhaps not express himself in public like this, but as an evangelical I am willing simply to look at the road map he has unfolded and, with full consciousness of all lingering problems, say, *soli Deo gloria.*

Index